Highlights

The GREAT BIG BOOK OF REALLY HARD PUZZLES

HIGHLIGHTS PRESS

HONESDALE, PENNSYLVANIA

TABLE OF CONTENTS

TABLE OF CONTENTS

MATH & LOGIC PUZZLES

Logic Puzzles

Number Puzzles

IDENTIFY THE ALIEN

Find the Alien Who:

- has more than two ears
- doesn't have a hat or crown
- has tentacles
- is holding a snack
- doesn't have purple hair
- has fewer than four eyes

WORDS AND OBJECTS

Now these are some busy beavers! There are 8 WORDS hidden on this page that match the 8 OBJECTS hidden on the next page. Can you find them all?

Keep track of the names of the objects you find in the spaces below.

_ _ _ _   _ _ _ _ _

_ _ _ _ _   _ _ _

_ _ _ _ _   _ _ _

_ _ _ _   _ _ _ _ _ _ _ _ _ _ _

MAJESTIC CASTLE MAZE

Find a path from START to FINISH. Then find the flag, dragon,
castle guard, 2 bats, and ship with 3 sails.

FINISH

START

Art by Matt Lyon

SHELL WASH MEMORY

Quick! Study this page for 60 seconds. Then go to the top of the next page to test your memory. Be on the lookout for a hidden puzzle piece!

Art by Brian White

TEST YOUR MEMORY

Did you study the scene on the previous page? Now see if you can answer these questions. Circle your responses. No peeking!

1 How many animals are holding brushes?   3   2   1

2 What is the snail doing?

SCRUBBING THE TURTLE   SLEEPING   WAITING IN LINE

3 Which one of these items does NOT appear on the cover?

SPONGE   CLOTH   BUCKET

4 What is the correct color of this lizard?

5 Where is the hidden puzzle piece?

ON A TREE   ON THE GROUND   ON A TURTLE'S SHELL

MAKE A MOVE

Mr. and Mrs. Melody are planning to move into a new house. Mr. Melody is a music teacher and goes to the school 5 days a week. Mrs. Melody manages a music shop and works 6 days a week. Which house should they choose if they want to travel the fewest total miles to and from work each week?

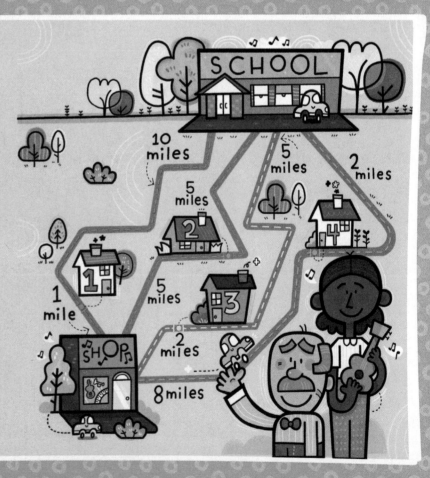

Art by Chris Eliopoulos

LOTS OF BOTS

There's an impostor hiding in this sea of robots. It's shiny, rectangular, and used to heat up slices of bread. Can you find it in the picture?

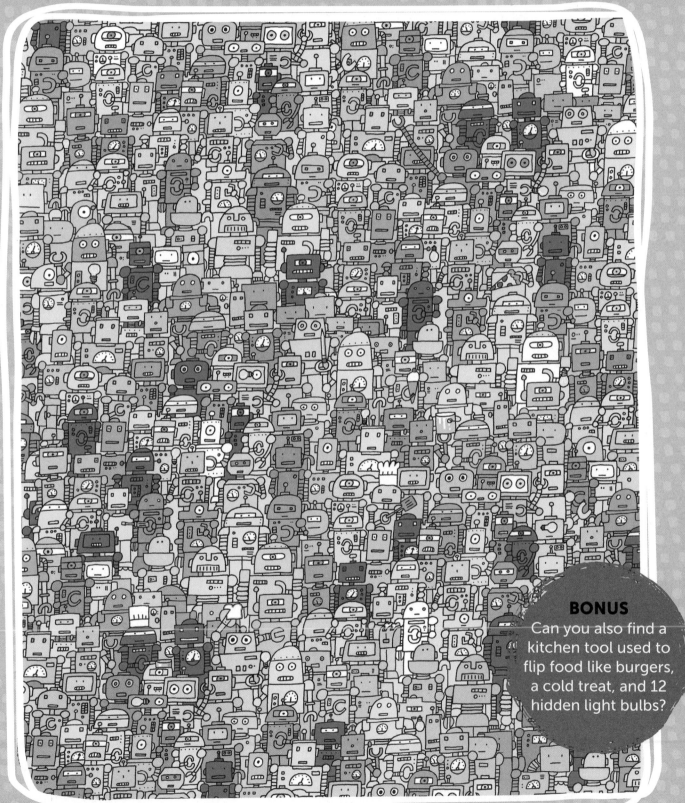

BONUS
Can you also find a kitchen tool used to flip food like burgers, a cold treat, and 12 hidden light bulbs?

Art by Travis Foster

TREE PLANTING

It's a beautiful day to plant a tree—and solve a puzzle! First, use the clues below to figure out the words. Each word is a hidden object to find in the big scene. Once you've found the 13 hidden objects, transfer the letters with numbers into the correct spaces on the next page to learn the answers to the riddles.

1. You put this on your hand to keep it warm.

__ __ __ __ __ __
     6

2. It glows in the night sky during part of each month.

__ __ __ __ __ __ __ __
  7   16

__ __ __ __
  11

3. You heat this in a toaster to make toast.

SLICE OF

__ __ __ __ __
      1

4. A _____ in a haystack

__ __ __ __ __ __ __
   15

5. You measure length with this.

__ __ __ __ __
17   8

6. You place a letter inside it.

__ __ __ __ __ __ __ __
            2

7. A queen might wear this.

__ __ __ __ __
  12

8. This beats inside your body.

__ __ __ __ __
   3

9. You need this to make a painting.

__ __ __ __ __ __
   10

__ __ __ __ __
14

10. It's often topped with cheese or pepperoni.

SLICE OF

__ __ __ __ __

11. Part of a sour, yellow fruit

WEDGE OF

__ __ __ __ __
  5

12. This handheld tool helps you see in the dark.

__ __ __ __ __ __ __ __ __ __
  4   13

13. Scrambled or sunny-side up

__ __ __
9

Art by Paula Becker

What kind of tree has hands?

$\underline{}$ $\underline{}\underline{}\underline{}\underline{}$ $\underline{}\underline{}\underline{}\underline{}$.
1 2 3 4 5 6 7 8 9

What kind of soda do trees drink?

$\underline{}\underline{}\underline{}\underline{}$ $\underline{}\underline{}\underline{}\underline{}$.
10 11 12 13 14 15 16 17

TURTLE CROSSING

This puzzle is crawling with 27 kinds of turtles. Their names fit into the grid in just one way. Use the number of letters in each word as a clue to where it might fit. No hurry. Take your time.

WORD LIST

3 LETTERS
BOG
BOX
MAP

4 LETTERS
MUSK
WOOD

5 LETTERS
BLACK
GREEN

7 LETTERS
PAINTED
SPOTTED

8 LETTERS
FALSE MAP
FLATBACK
SNAPPING
STINKPOT
TERRAPIN

9 LETTERS
BLANDING'S
HAWKSBILL
YELLOW MUD

10 LETTERS
EASTERN MUD
LOGGERHEAD
POND SLIDER

11 LETTERS
KEMP'S RIDLEY
LEATHERBACK
OLIVE RIDLEY
RIVER COOTER

14 LETTERS
RED-EARED
SLIDER
SPINY
SOFTSHELL

15 LETTERS
SMOOTH
SOFTSHELL

XING

SLOW

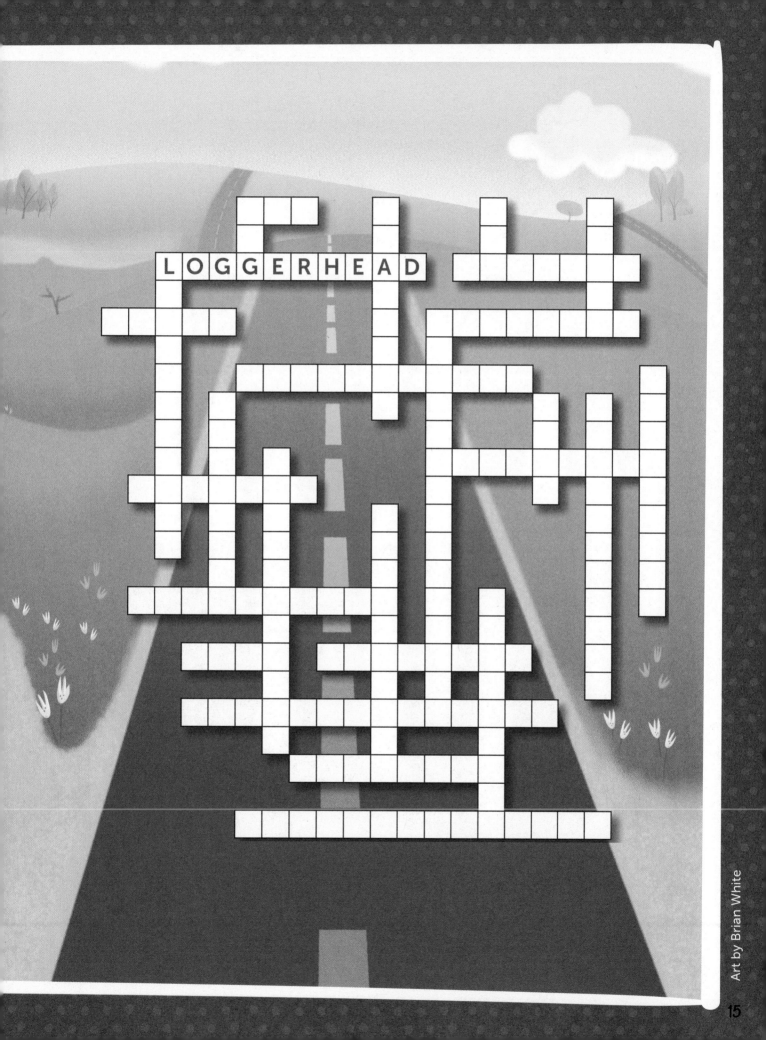

LOGGERHEAD

GRIN AND BEAR IT

Can you pick out the 20 bears hiding in this carrot crop?

BRING ON THE BLING

This outdoor theater performance is filled with shiny bling! There are also nine objects or actions in the scene that rhyme with BLING. Each of these nine words only has one syllable (so **running** or **sitting** don't count). Can you find them all?

THIS OTTER BE FUN

There are 14 sea otters floating in these grids. Using the directions and hints below, can you figure out where all the sea otters go?

Look at the grids. Each numbered square tells you how many of the empty squares touching it (above, below, left, right, or diagonally) contain a sea otter. Write an X on squares that can't have a sea otter. Then write SO on squares that have a sea otter.

HINTS:
- An otter cannot go in a square that has a number.
- Put an X on all the squares touching a zero.
- Even if you're not sure where to put all the otters connected to a number, fill in the ones you are sure of. (Look at what's not possible based on the other numbered squares. Try it with a pencil and eraser.)

This grid has 4 otters.

1			
	1		1
1		1	
	2		

This grid has 10 otters.

2			0		1
1		4			1
1		2		4	

SUPER CHALLENGE!

These animals are taking their time scaling the cliffside.
Without clues or knowing what to look for, can you
find the 25 hidden objects in this scene?

BONUS
Say this three times, fast:
Critters climbing rocky cliffs.

Art by Brian Michael Weaver

OCEAN EXPLORATIONS

Find your way from the ocean surface to the seafloor by answering each question. The right answers will take you through the maze from START to FINISH. The wrong answers will lead you to a dead end.

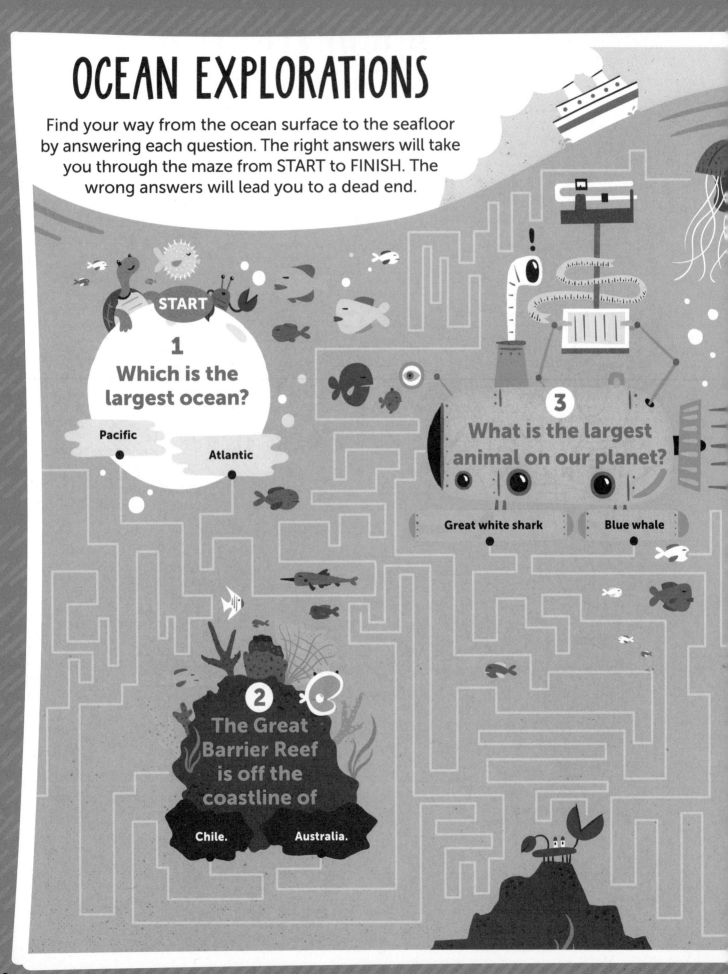

START

1
Which is the largest ocean?

Pacific

Atlantic

3
What is the largest animal on our planet?

Great white shark

Blue whale

2
The Great Barrier Reef is off the coastline of

Chile.

Australia.

5 How many hearts does an octopus have?

2 hearts   3 hearts

6 The Pacific Ocean is circled by the "Ring of Fire." Why is it called the Ring of Fire?

Because the sun setting on the ocean looks like fire

Because there are active volcanoes around this ocean

7 How many plant and wildlife species in the ocean do scientists say we may have yet to discover?

9 million   9 billion

4 Which ocean is the warmest?

Indian   Pacific

8 What is the deepest place in the ocean called?

Deep Challenge

Challenger Deep

FINISH

THE *HOLE* SHEBANG

Bakers once made a 3,739-pound doughnut.

Doughnuts have been around for centuries.

24

Each doughnut has an exact match—except one.
Can you find the one without a match?

Spudnuts are doughnuts made from potatoes.

POLAR PATTERNS

Find each pattern below in the grid.

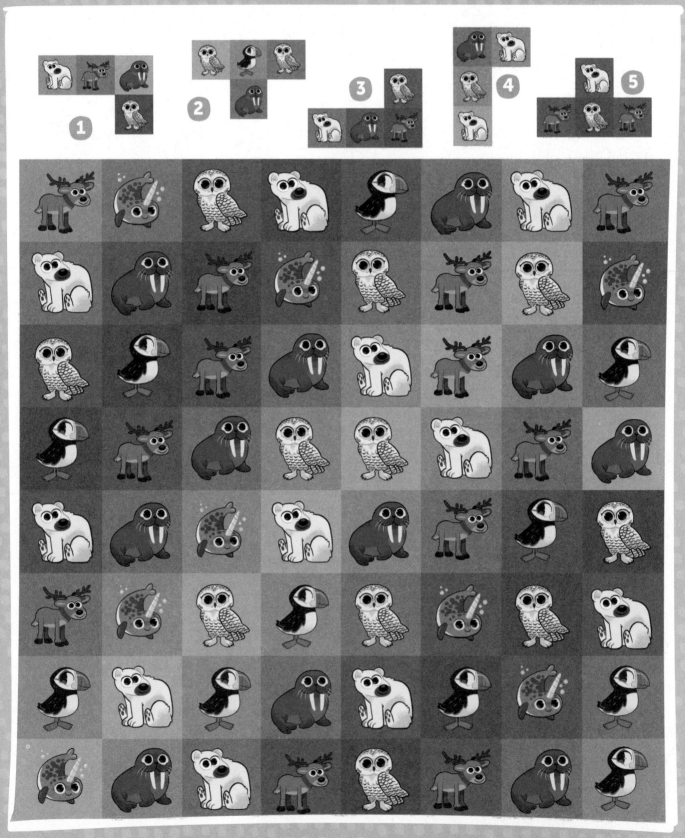

Art by Erin Hunting

BLACK AND WHITE

Can you find the camera, television, chess game, magic wand, cat, playing card, zebra, soccer ball, earmuffs, tuxedo, skunk, newspaper, Dalmatian, baseball cap, and eight-ball?

BONUS
Find five black-and-white cookies.

Art by Brian Michael Weaver

Each of these small scenes contains 6 hidden objects from the list below. Some objects are hidden in more than one scene. Can you find the 6 hidden objects in each scene?

HIDDEN OBJECT LIST

adhesive bandage (5)
carrot (2)
comb (4)
crescent moon (4)
envelope (4)
feather (2)
hockey stick (3)
piece of popcorn (4)
pitcher (2)
screw (2)
slice of pizza (2)
waffle (2)

The numbers tell you how many times each object is hidden.

BONUS
Two scenes contain the exact same set of hidden objects. Can you find that matching pair?

Art by Brian Michael Weaver

FLOWER POWER

Instead of working across and down, you work clockwise or counterclockwise in this petal puzzle. Each clue matches a numbered petal. Start your answer at the number and work toward the center of the flower.

CLOCKWISE

1. Dirt
2. You do this on a phone.
3. A pretty flower with thorns
4. A little wet
5. A rake, spade, or shovel
6. A single bit of rain
7. _____ on the cob
8. A type of fish; rhymes with sharp
9. They help with weeding.
10. A red root vegetable
11. Chaser of the three pigs
12. A group of ballplayers
13. Beef and pork
14. To loan
15. A feathered flyer
16. To install on a computer
17. Gardener's enemy
18. Lima, kidney, or string

COUNTERCLOCKWISE

1. A plant's beginning
2. Froglike creature
3. Water from the sky
4. Barbie or Raggedy Ann
5. Small job
6. Rounded building top
7. A field's yield
8. Chilled
9. Stringed instrument
10. Your birthday marks the day you were _____.
11. A word that means "to cry"
12. You have five on each foot.
13. What ice will do in the sun
14. Food-making part of a plant
15. A flashlight sends a _____ of light.
16. Clothes dryer's fuzzy leftovers
17. Each puzzle answer is one _____.
18. Part of a necklace

HIDE-AND-SEEK

These foxes found some good hiding places! See if you can find all 16 hidden objects in the scene below.

Now look for 10 differences between the nearly identical scenes on these two pages.

Art by Lee Cosgrove

ON YOUR FEET

There are 29 different foot words and phrases hidden in this grid. For each one, the word FOOT has been replaced with 🐾. Look up, down, across, backward, and diagonally.

WORD LIST

BAREFOOT

BEST FOOT
FORWARD

BIGFOOT

CROWFOOT

FLATFOOT

FOOT FAULT

FOOT THE BILL

FOOTBALL

FOOTBATH

FOOTBRIDGE

FOOTGEAR

FOOTHILL

FOOTHOLD

FOOTLIGHT

FOOTLOCKER

FOOTLOOSE

FOOTMAN

FOOTNOTE

FOOTPATH

FOOTPRINT

FOOTRACE

FOOTREST

FOOTSTEP

FOOTSTOOL

FOOTWORK

HOTFOOT

SURE-FOOTED

TENDERFOOT

UNDERFOOT

```
T H E D   F A U L T   B
T S L P L L L I H   E L E N
N E T L   L O T R E N O S
I R F O I L A H E   D O T
R   R   O B O B   N E S
P E T S   L E C   O R E F
  O   P A T H H K T   S O
H T O   W O R C T E     R
R G M U N D E R     R W W
O A B A   L I G H T A O A
N R E   B R I D G E C R R
E F O G O B A R E   E K D
S U R E   E D F L A T   T
```

TRIVIA QUESTION:

Why doesn't a bear wear socks?

Put the uncircled letters in order on the blanks.

__ __   __ __ __ __ __ __ __   __ __   __ __

__ __ __ __ __ __ __ __ __.

Art by Erin Hunting (bear)

WORDS AND OBJECTS

There are 8 WORDS hidden on this page that match the
8 OBJECTS hidden on the next page. Can you find them all?

Keep track of the names of the objects you find in the spaces below.

— — — —

— — — — — — —

— — — — — — — — — — — — — —

— — — — —

— — — — — —

— — — —

— — — — — — — — —

— — — — — —

GRAND CANYON

Maya and her dad need to catch up to their family.
Can you help them find the right path?

Art by Luisa Uribe

BONUS
How many miles will Syd have traveled once he returns home?

D

LIBRARY

1.5 MI

1.5 MI

BUSY BIKING

Syd is having a yard sale. He wants to hang signs along each street and in each building. Help him find a path that:

- Starts and ends at home (A).
- Goes to the pharmacy first.
- Does not go down the same street more than once.

HINT: It's OK to pass by the same building more than once.

A

E

PHARMACY

1.5 MI

0.5 MI

1 MI

1 MI

0.5 MI

0.5 MI

FLORIST

POST OFFICE

0.5 MI

MARKET

B

C

F

Art by Shaw Nielsen

BALLPARK MEMORY

Quick! Study this page for 60 seconds. Then go to the top of the next page to test your memory. Be on the lookout for a hidden puzzle piece!

Art by Brian Michael Weaver

TEST YOUR MEMORY

Did you study the scene on the previous page? Now see if you can answer these questions. Circle your responses. No peeking!

1 How many kids in the scene are wearing glasses?   4   2   3

2 What team is the crowd rooting for?

THE ROCKETS   THE JETS   THE ASTROS

3 What is the correct color of this boy's baseball cap?

4 How many eyes does the alien have?   3   2   1

5 Where is the hidden puzzle piece?

ON THE SEATS   IN THE TREES   ON THE SPACESHIP

ANITA'S PITAS

Anita Aardvark sells bags of pitas for $4.00 per bag. After today's sales, how many bags of pitas did she sell? How much money did she make? Use the clues below to figure out the answers to these questions.

CLUES
- Ruthie Rhino bought 12 bags.
- Hector Hippo paid $12.00 for his bags.
- Ellie Elephant bought twice as many bags as Ruthie.
- Glen Giraffe paid $28.00 less than Ellie paid.

BONUS
Anita lost her measuring cups. Can you find all 5 of them?

HEN FRENZY

There's an impostor hiding in this hectic henhouse. It bleats, has a beard, and likes to climb. Can you find it in the picture?

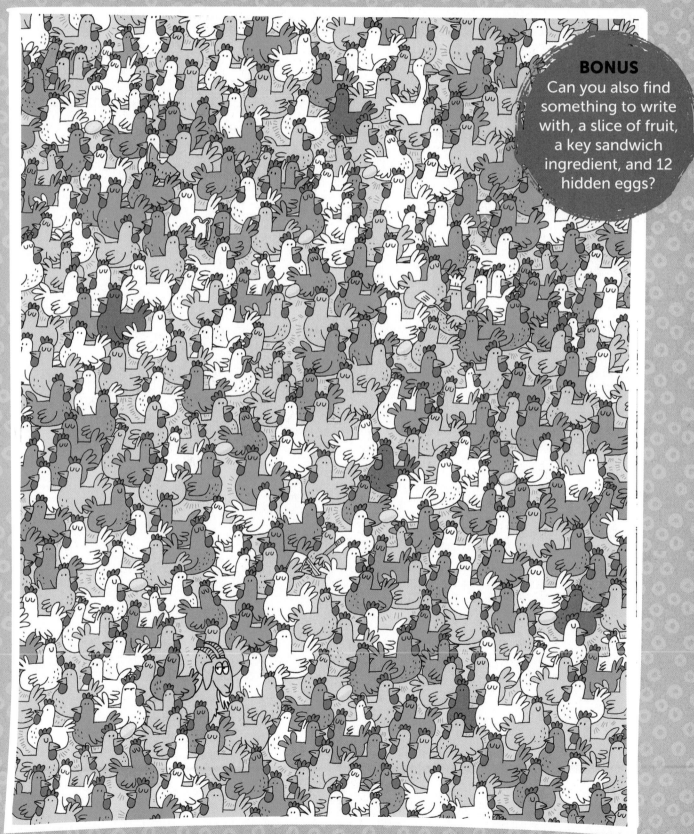

BONUS
Can you also find something to write with, a slice of fruit, a key sandwich ingredient, and 12 hidden eggs?

Art by Travis Foster

NATURE'S NIGHT LIGHTS

The twinkling fireflies in this scene may be easy to spot—but the hidden objects in the picture are not! First use the secret code to figure out what objects are hidden in the scene. Then use the list to find the 18 hidden objects in the big picture.

1. X Z M — `C` `A` `N`

2. X Z M W B · X Z M V

3. R X V - X I V Z N · X L M V

4. Y F G G L M

5. Z R I K O Z M V

6. H K L L M

7. Z K K O V

8. O R T S G · Y F O Y

9. N Z T M R U B R M T · T O Z H H

10. U L I P

11. X O L X P

12. D V W T V · L U · O V N L M

13. X I L D M

14. Y Z M Z M Z

15. T O L E V

16. I F O V I

17. N Z T R X · O Z N K

18. V M E V O L K V

CODE CRACKER

A=Z	E=V	I=R	M=N	Q=J	U=F	Y=B
B=Y	F=U	J=Q	N=M	R=I	V=E	Z=A
C=X	G=T	K=P	O=L	S=H	W=D	
D=W	H=S	L=O	P=K	T=G	X=C	

44

WHAT'S FOR LUNCH?

The names of 35 lunches can fit into this crisscross grid.
Chow down and try to fit them all in!

3 LETTERS
DAL
LOX
PHO

4 LETTERS
GYRO
RIBS
TACO

5 LETTERS
CHILI
CURRY
PIZZA
RAMEN
SUSHI

6 LETTERS
BURGER
OMELET
PB AND J
QUICHE

7 LETTERS
BURRITO
FALAFEL
LASAGNA
PORK BBQ

8 LETTERS
EGG SALAD
EMPANADA
TUNA MELT

9 LETTERS
CHEF SALAD
SLOPPY JOE
SPAGHETTI

10 LETTERS
FISH STICKS
QUESADILLA
TOMATO SOUP
VEGGIE WRAP

11 LETTERS
HAM SANDWICH
MEATBALL SUB

12 LETTERS
CHICKEN WINGS
MAC AND CHEESE
RICE AND BEANS

13 LETTERS
GRILLED CHEESE

D A L

Art by Mitch Mortimer

COME CLOSER

Can you spot 23 caterpillars on this leaf?

RIDDLE SUDOKU

Our Sudoku puzzles use letters instead of numbers.

Fill in the squares so the six letters appear only once in each row, column, and 2 × 3 box. Then read the highlighted squares to find the answer to each riddle.

LETTERS: I L E O K N

				K	
		L		N	
E	K		O		
		I		E	N
	E		I		
L				O	

What does a pig call its mother's brother?

Answer: _ _ _ _ _ _ .

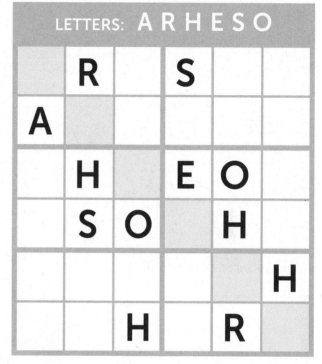

LETTERS: A R H E S O

	R		S		
A					
	H		E		O
	S	O		H	
					H
	H			R	

What do you call a sick pony?

Answer:
A little _ _ _ _ _ _ .

FARM ANIMAL HEAD-SCRATCHERS

Read the sets of clues to figure out who the two animals are.

1. If you hang out with me and my flock, you'll have a *woolly* good time! And if you can't fall asleep, you can count on me to help. Who am I?

2. I have a comb but no hair. And here's something to crow about: I make a great alarm clock in the early morning! Who am I?

49

LOOK UP!

There are 14 UFOs hidden in these grids. Using the directions and hints below, can you figure out where all the UFOs go?

Look at the grids. Each numbered square tells you how many of the empty squares touching it (above, below, left, right, or diagonally) have a UFO. Write an **X** on squares that can't have a UFO. Then write **UFO** on squares that have a UFO.

HINTS:

- Write an *X* on all the squares touching a zero.
- Look in the corners where a numbered square may make it more obvious where a UFO is hiding.
- A UFO cannot go in a square that has a number.

This grid has 4 UFOs.

		3	
2			2
	2		
0			0

This grid has 10 UFOs.

	1			1
		2		
2				1
	6		4	
				2
0		1	3	

Art by Real-illusioin/istock (alien); Photo by Oriontrail/istock (background)

MITTEN MATCH

Find 8 lost mittens in the scene.
Then find the person who lost each mitten.

BONUS
Unscramble the letters below for another winter weather clothing item: **FRASC**

Art by Paula Becker

SUPER CHALLENGE!

It's a gorgeous day for a hike! Hit the trail and see if you can find all the hidden objects.

- adhesive bandage
- arrow
- artist's brush
- baseball bat
- bell
- book
- boot
- car
- coat hanger
- crown
- drumstick
- envelope
- fish
- glove
- hockey stick
- horseshoe
- mitten
- needle
- paper clip
- sailboat
- saucepan
- slice of pizza
- sock
- toothbrush
- wedge of lime
- wishbone

BONUS
Can you find 5 birds in this scene?

Art by Dave Klug

53

QUIZOPOLIS

Hop aboard for the city tour! Cruise from START to FINISH by answering each question correctly.

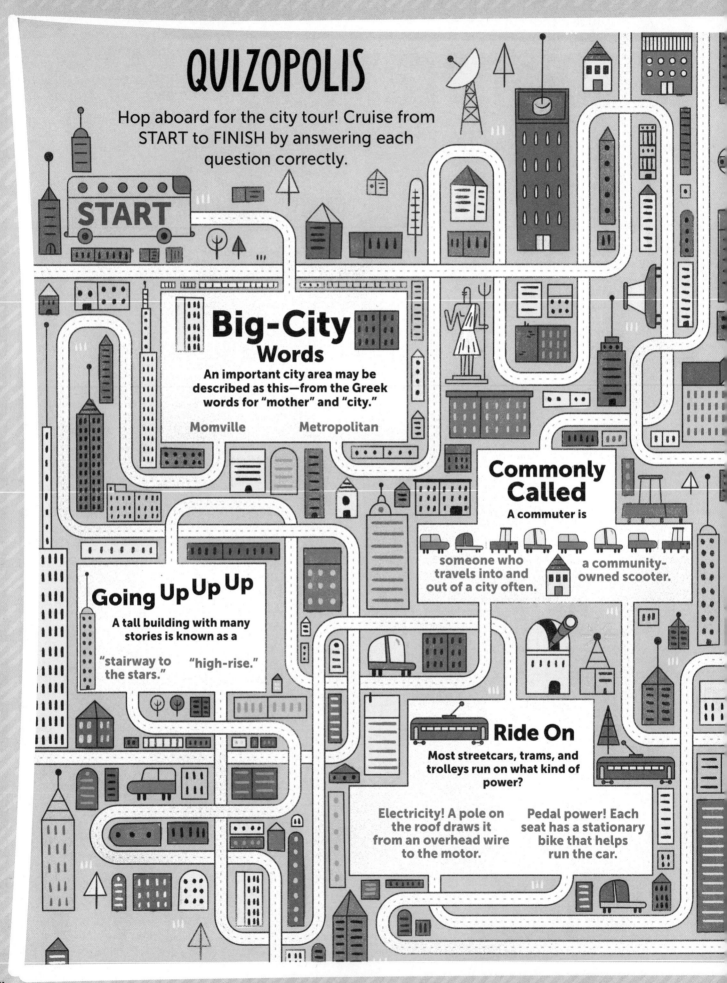

START

Big-City Words

An important city area may be described as this—from the Greek words for "mother" and "city."

Momville   Metropolitan

Commonly Called

A commuter is

someone who travels into and out of a city often.

a community-owned scooter.

Going Up Up Up

A tall building with many stories is known as a

"stairway to the stars."   "high-rise."

Ride On

Most streetcars, trams, and trolleys run on what kind of power?

Electricity! A pole on the roof draws it from an overhead wire to the motor.

Pedal power! Each seat has a stationary bike that helps run the car.

Puppy Place

A dog park is

where dogs go to take catnaps.

where people take their dogs to play off-leash.

That's Sup-"urb"

An urban area is a densely developed region, often with many people. *Urban* comes from the Latin word for

"herb garden."

"city."

Stars on the Street

Another name for a musician or other entertainer who works for donations is

an avenue actor.

a busker.

Exit to Exhibits

Where would you be more likely to see gemstones, ancient tools, and dinosaur fossils?

See 'em in a museum of natural history.

Find 'em at a football field.

Tuck It Away

A pocket park is

a terrarium-to-go, made by sticking moss in your pocket.

a small public outdoor space, often between buildings in a city.

FINISH

SUBWAY

FOOD FEST

Find each pattern below in the grid.

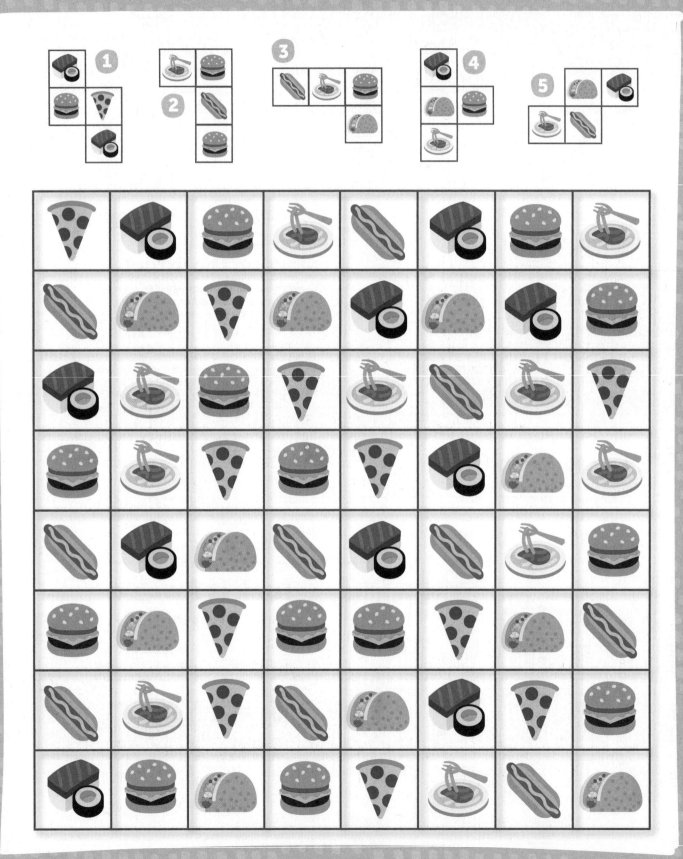

Art by Getty

SCIENCE RULES!

Find 7 calculators, 6 magnets, 5 planets, 4 microscopes, 3 pairs of lab goggles, 2 books, and 1 telescope.

BONUS
Find two matching robots.

Art by Chris Piascik

Each of these small scenes contains 6 hidden objects from the list below. Some objects are hidden in more than one scene. Can you find the 6 hidden objects in each scene?

HIDDEN OBJECT LIST

banana (3)
boomerang (3)
envelope (2)
eyeglasses (2)
fork (2)
glove (4)
magnet (4)
pencil (5)
ring (3)
slice of pizza (4)
waffle (2)
wedge of orange (2)

BONUS
Two scenes contain the exact same set of hidden objects. Can you find that matching pair?

The numbers tell you how many times each object is hidden.

GOING IN CIRCLES

Go around and around using the clues to fill in the spaces. The last letter of each word will also be the first letter of the next word.

1. Our planet
5. Bees make this sweet treat.
9. There are 365 days in one.
12. It controls the TV.
17. A hen lays one.
19. Brown sauce for meat
23. Color of a banana or lemon
28. The coldest season
33. Famous place for presidents: Mount _____
40. Where the sun rises
43. A magician's feat
47. A baby cat
52. What squirrels hide
55. A frozen friend
61. A bird builds it.
64. It runs on tracks.
68. Opposite of south
72. Where you live
76. Computer message
81. Opposite of tight
85. Animal with a trunk
93. Opposite of false
96. Opposite of exit
100. Color of some fire engines
102. Third meal of the day
107. A magician pulls this out of a hat.
112. Fairy-tale finish: _____ _____

Why is
a circle
always hot?

Because it's
360 degrees.

Art by Jim Steck

A FINE EVENING

Throw on your finest frock, then see if you can find all
12 hidden objects in the party scene below.

Now look for 10 differences between the nearly identical scenes on these two pages.

Art by Jef Czekaj

A WHOLE DIFFERENT ANIMAL

There are more animals here than meet the eye. The numbered scenes can each be described by three words. The first letters of these three words spell out the name of an animal. For example, the first scene is DONKEY ORGANIZING GLASSES. The first three letters spell DOG. The other scenes spell out: ANT, BAT, BEE, CAT, COW, EEL, PIG and RAT. See if you can match these animal names to each scene below.

SHE SELLS SEASHELLS

Celia is searching for seashells to sell by the seashore. Her pail can hold 25 shells, and she wants to fill it up on her way back to her booth. Figure out the sequence of paths from START to FINISH that totals exactly 25 seashells without going on the same path twice. The crabs help Celia remember how many shells she's picked up on each path.

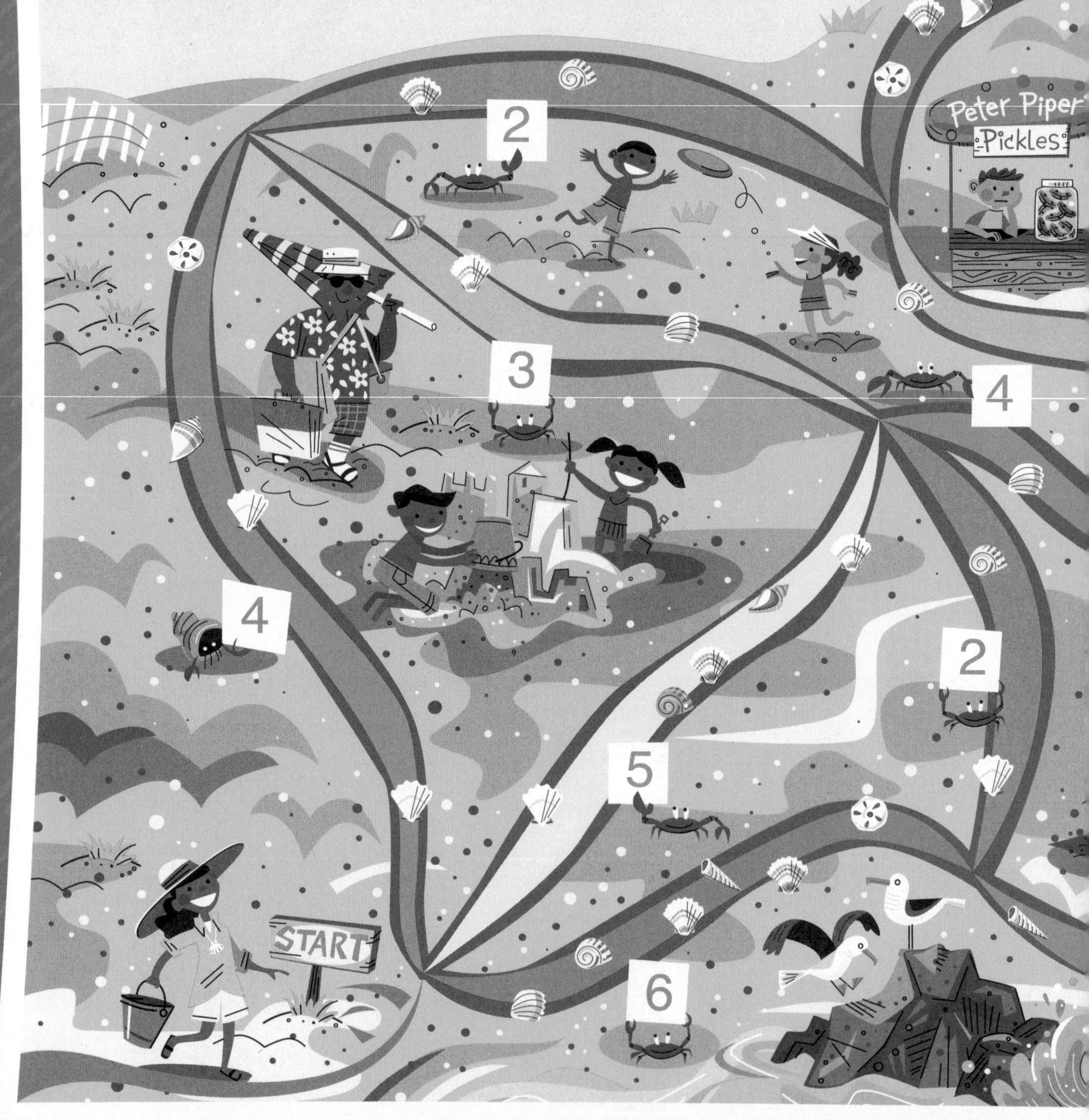

2

3

4

4

2

5

6

Peter Piper Pickles

START

HINT: When trying a route, keep a running seashell total in your head or on a piece of paper. If you end up with too low or high a number, try a different sequence of paths.

WORDS AND OBJECTS

Whoosh! All the animals look on as the orangutan jets down the zipline. There are 8 WORDS hidden on this page that match the 8 OBJECTS hidden on the next page. Can you find them all?

Keep track of the names of the objects you find in the spaces below.

_ _ _   _ _ _ _

_ _ _ _ _   _ _ _ _ _

_ _ _ _ _   _ _ , _ _ _ _ _

_ _ _ _ _   _ _ _ _ _ _ _ _ _

GALLERY VISIT

Make your way around the paintings from START to FINISH.

BONUS
Find 8 paintbrushes.

Art by Jennifer Harney

ROAD TRIP MEMORY

Quick! Study this page for 60 seconds. Then go to the top of the next page to test your memory. Be on the lookout for a hidden puzzle piece!

Art by Brian White

TEST YOUR MEMORY

Did you study the scene on the previous page? Now see if you can answer these questions. Circle your responses. No peeking!

1. How many dogs are in the car?   3   4   5

2. What is on the license plate?   GRRRR   ARFFF   RUFFFF

3. What color is the butterfly?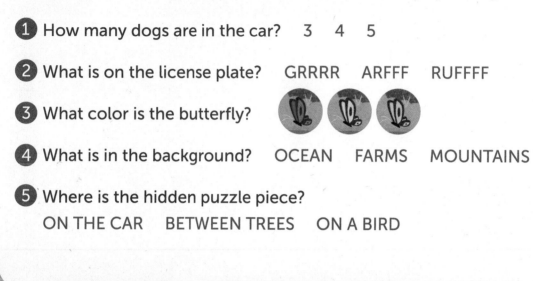

4. What is in the background?   OCEAN   FARMS   MOUNTAINS

5. Where is the hidden puzzle piece?
   ON THE CAR   BETWEEN TREES   ON A BIRD

IF AT FIRST...

The answer to the riddle below is easy if you know your measurements. Each "if" statement will give you a letter and tell you where to put it. Fill in all the letters and you will have your answer.

1. If a tablespoon is larger than a teaspoon, the first letter is a C. If not, it is a D.

2. If there are 36 inches in a yard, the second and ninth letters are O. If not they are A.

3. If there are two pints in a quart, the tenth letter is a U. If not, the fifth letter is a U.

4. If there are 6,000 feet in a mile, letters 3, 4, and 8 are T. If not, they are L.

5. If there are 1,000 meters in a kilometer, letter 11 is an R. If not, it is an S.

6. If a millimeter is smaller than a centimeter, the sixth letter is an E. If not it is an R.

7. If a ton is more than 1,000 pounds, the seventh letter is an F. If not, it is a B.

8. If a meter is longer than a foot, the fifth letter is an I. If not, the tenth letter is an I.

WHAT DO YOU CALL DOUGH USED FOR MAKING DOG BISCUITS?

___ ___ ___ ___ ___ ___   ___ ___ ___ ___ ___ .
1   2   3   4   5   6   7   8   9   10 11

PENGUIN POSEUR

There's an impostor hiding in this pack of penguins. It has udders and spots and usually hangs out with a herd. Can you find it in the picture?

BONUS
Can you also find a snoozing bird, a cheesy snack, and 13 hidden fish?

Art by Travis Foster

SPOOKY STORYTELLING

You're invited to a sleepover with spooky stories—and hidden objects! First use the clues below to figure out the words. Each word is a hidden object to find in the big scene. Once you've found the 12 hidden objects, transfer the letters with numbers into the correct spaces on the next page to learn the answers to the riddles.

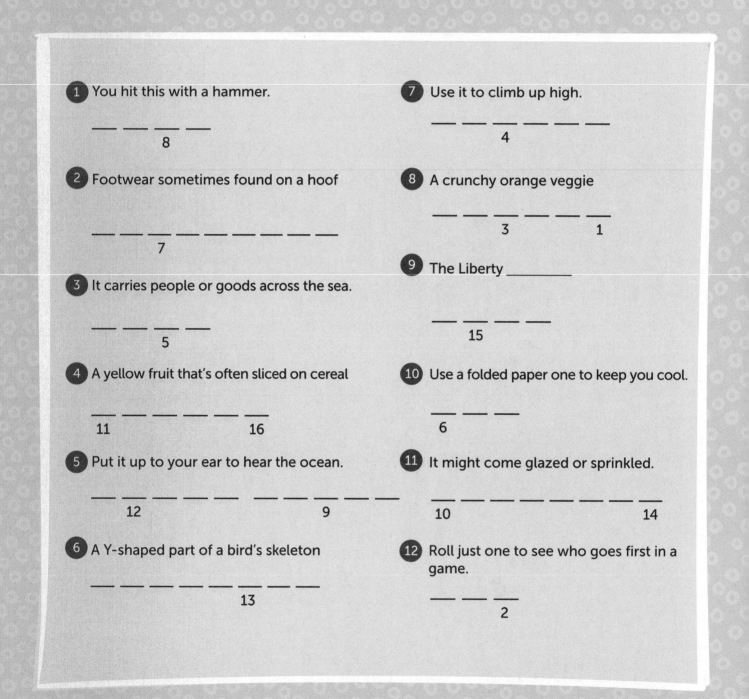

1 You hit this with a hammer.

___ ___ ___ ___
　　　　8

2 Footwear sometimes found on a hoof

___ ___ ___ ___ ___ ___ ___ ___ ___
　　　　7

3 It carries people or goods across the sea.

___ ___ ___ ___
　　　5

4 A yellow fruit that's often sliced on cereal

___ ___ ___ ___ ___ ___
11　　　　　　16

5 Put it up to your ear to hear the ocean.

___ ___ ___ ___ ___　___ ___ ___ ___ ___
　12　　　　　　　　9

6 A Y-shaped part of a bird's skeleton

___ ___ ___ ___ ___ ___ ___ ___
　　　　　13

7 Use it to climb up high.

___ ___ ___ ___ ___ ___
　　　4

8 A crunchy orange veggie

___ ___ ___ ___ ___ ___
　　　3　　　1

9 The Liberty _____

___ ___ ___ ___
　　15

10 Use a folded paper one to keep you cool.

___ ___ ___ ___
　6

11 It might come glazed or sprinkled.

___ ___ ___ ___ ___ ___ ___ ___
10　　　　　　　　14

12 Roll just one to see who goes first in a game.

___ ___ ___ ___
　　2

How do ghosts take their eggs?

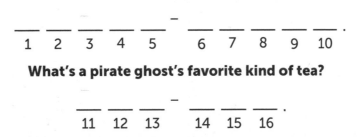

__ __ __ __ __ – __ __ __ __ __ .
1   2   3   4   5   6   7   8   9 10

What's a pirate ghost's favorite kind of tea?

__ __ __ – __ __ __ .
11 12 13   14 15 16

DOGGONE IT!

The 30 kinds of dogs listed here fit into the grid in just one way. Can you fetch them all?

3 LETTERS
PUG

5 LETTERS
BOXER
CORGI
HUSKY

6 LETTERS
AFGHAN
BEAGLE
COLLIE
POODLE

7 LETTERS
BULLDOG
MASTIFF
PIT BULL
SAMOYED
SPANIEL
TERRIER

8 LETTERS
DOBERMAN
SHEEPDOG
SHEPHERD

9 LETTERS
CHIHUAHUA
DACHSHUND
DALMATIAN
GREAT DANE
GREYHOUND
PEKINGESE
RETRIEVER
SCHNAUZER

10 LETTERS
BLOODHOUND
WEIMARANER

11 LETTERS
BASSET HOUND
IRISH SETTER

12 LETTERS
SAINT BERNARD

LOTS OF LUCK

Can you find the
25 horseshoes
hiding in this
canyon?

REACH FOR THE STARS

There are so many stars in the night sky! Circle the 30 words or phrases containing STAR hidden in this grid. The word STAR has been replaced with a ★. Look up, down, across, backward, and diagonally. The uncircled letters answer the trivia question.

WORD LIST

CORNSTARCH	STAR ANISE	STARLIGHT
CUSTARD	STAR MAP	STARLING
DASTARDLY	STAR FRUIT	STARSHIP
KICK-START	STAR POWER	STARSTRUCK
LODESTAR	STAR-STUDDED	STARTUP
LUCKY STARS	STARBOARD	STARVE
MEGASTAR	STARBURST	SUPERSTAR
MOVIE STAR	STARDOM	WISH UPON
MUSTARD	STARDUST	A STAR
POLESTAR	STARFISH	
ROCK STAR	STARGAZE	

```
★ B O A R D I D A ★ D L Y
E T H G I L ★ ★ S H I P P
D T S N S U P E R ★ O A T
O ★ L U C K Y ★ S L M A R
L K A ★ A N I S E ★ D O ★
T C K N S T A ★ R E C F D
R I C T O A T A D K I ★ H
E K U S S P E D ★ S U L C
W ★ R R L U U Z H M I M ★
O L T U F T D H A T E S N
P I S B S ★ A ★ S G V M R
★ N ★ ★ ★ D O M A I ★ E O
T G M O V I E ★ E O W R C
```

TRIVIA QUESTION:
What is a shooting star?
Put the uncircled letters in order on the blanks.

ANSWER:

It __ __ __'__ __ __ __ __ __ __ __

__ __ __. __ __, __ __ __ __ __ __ __.

A BERRY SPECIAL PUZZLE

There are 14 blueberries hidden in these grids. Using the directions and hints below, can you figure out where all the blueberries go?

Look at the grids. Each numbered square tells you how many of the empty squares touching it (above, below, left, right, or diagonally) contain a blueberry. Write an X on squares that can't have a blueberry. Then write a B on squares that have a blueberry.

HINTS:

- A berry cannot go in a square that has a number.

- Put an X on all the squares touching a zero.

- Even if you're not sure where to put all the blueberries connected to a number, fill in the ones you are sure of.

- Remember how many blueberries you have to find for each puzzle.

This pancake has 4 blueberries.

			0
2			
		3	
	3		1

This pancake has 10 blueberries.

	2		2	
				1
	3		6	
				1
	3		2	
2				1

Photos by Ryanjlane/istock (pancakes); Rimblow/istock (blueberries)

GO FISH

Each fish has an exact match—except one.
Can you find the one without a match?

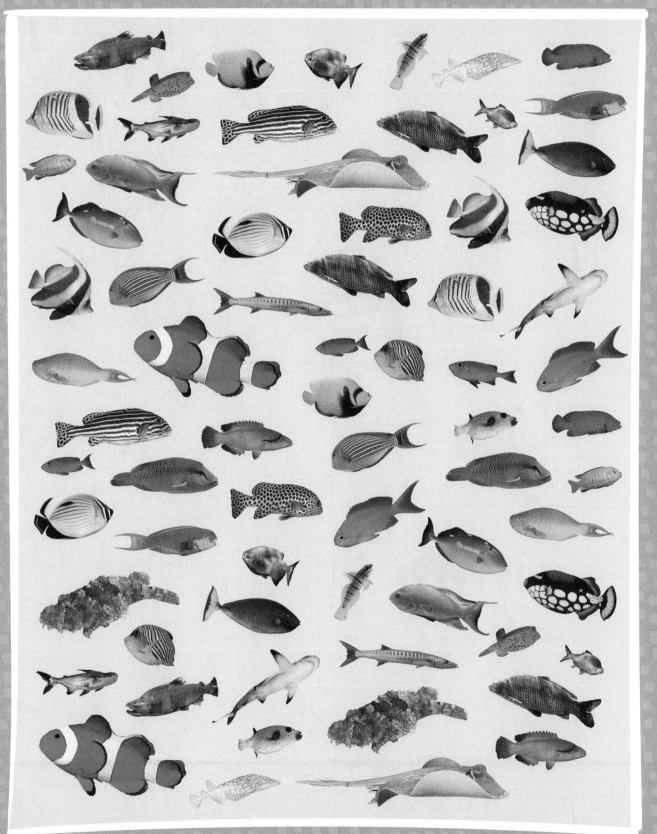

SUPER CHALLENGE!

Everyone in this city has got something to sing about today. Without clues or knowing what to look for, can you find the 24 hidden objects in this scene?

Art by Paula Becker

TAKE A WALK IN THE PARK

Hike from START to FINISH by answering each question correctly.

START

Nature Rocks

In Utah's Bryce Canyon National Park, you can find _____, which are rock deposits that have been lifted and sculpted by nature.

hoodoos   hoodon'ts

Tops in Tourism

With over 11 million annual visitors in an average year, what is the most-visited national park in the U.S.?

Grand Canyon National Park

(Arizona)

Great Smoky Mountains National Park

(North Carolina and Tennessee)

All Who Wander

This national park has the French word for "traveler" in its name because the French used the surrounding waterways for fur trading 250 years ago.

Everglades National Park

(Florida)

Voyageurs National Park

(Minnesota)

A Whole Lot of Land

This state has over 54 million acres of national parks—the same size as Utah!

Texas — Alaska

Amazing Architects

Ancestral Pueblo people lived in structures built into the cliffs of what would later become this national park.

Yosemite National Park (California) — — Mesa Verde National Park (Colorado)

Hello, Neighbor!

Cuyahoga Valley National Park is about 20 miles away from which city?

Cleveland, Ohio — — Philadelphia, Pennsylvania

See You There!

U.S. national parks host _____ visitors in an average year. That's almost the number of people who live in the U.S.

318 million — 70 million

Special Species

More than 90 percent of the native plants and animals found in this state's national parks cannot be found anywhere else on Earth!

Hawai'i — Alaska

A Trio of Parks

This California mountain range is home to three national parks.

Blue Ridge Mountains — — Sierra Nevada

FINISH

Art by Mario Zucca

MAGICAL CREATURE COMBOS

Find each pattern below in the grid.

AWESOME BLOSSOMS

Find 4 shamrocks, 4 butterflies, 6 dragonflies, and a purple beetle.

Art by Pintachan

Each of these small scenes contains 6 hidden objects from the list below. Some objects are hidden in more than one scene. Can you find the 6 hidden objects in each scene?

HIDDEN OBJECT LIST

boomerang (3)
candle (3)
glove (3)
lollipop (2)
magnet (3)
needle (3)
pencil (4)
slice of cake (3)
slice of pizza (3)
snail (3)
spoon (3)
waffle (3)

BONUS
Two scenes contain the exact same set of hidden objects. Can you find that matching pair?

The numbers tell you how many times each object is hidden.

DINO-SOUR LEMONADE

SUPER SAURUS STORE

Art by Brian Michael Weaver

PASTA SALT AND PEPPER

Every answer in this puzzle is made up of letters from the phrase SPAGHETTI AND MEATBALLS. Use your noodle to twirl them all!

ACROSS

1. Hit a homerun with this.
2. One of the five senses
5. "Pretty _____ with a cherry on top"
8. Baked pasta dinner
10. Astros or Steelers
12. Angry
13. A bone between the waist and the thigh
14. UFO driver
15. Quiet
16. Don't forget to floss these.
18. It goes with green eggs.
19. Bigger than a quiz
21. Dinner might go on this.
24. A to Z
27. Earth is the third one from the sun.
29. Open-toed shoes
30. Place surrounded by water
31. A doctor for 16 Across

DOWN

1. The Nutcracker is a famous one.
3. Square, triangle, or circle
4. Cellar
6. Animal with a trunk
7. Put this on an envelope.
9. Win this at the Olympics.
11. Not at school
14. Professional sports player
15. A big boat
17. Name of a book
20. "The Star-_____ Banner"
22. Mountains in Switzerland
23. Backbone
25. Marching or concert
26. Oak or beech
28. Goes with pepper

DEER DASH

The race is on for these deer. As they make their way to the finish line, see if you can find all 17 hidden objects in the scene below.

Now look for 11 differences between the nearly identical scenes on these two pages.

Art by Gary LaCoste

RIDDLE SUDOKU

Fill in the squares so the six letters appear only once in each row, column, and 2 × 3 box. Then read the highlighted squares to find the answer to each riddle.

LETTERS: A C H L N U

				N	
		C		U	
H	N				
				H	U
	H		A		
	C			L	

What's an astronaut's favorite meal?

Answer: __ __ __ __ __ __.

LETTERS: O T E R C K

	K		E		
C					
	R		T		O
	E	O		R	
					R
	R		K		

What only starts to work after it's fired?

Answer:

A __ __ __ __ __ __.

WORD FOR WORDS

The letters in INTERSTELLAR can be used to make many other words. Use clues below to come up with some of them.

1. A hot drink __ __ __

2. What we breathe __ __ __

3. A snakelike fish __ __ __

4. Someone who doesn't tell the truth __ __ __ __ __

5. Another word for story __ __ __ __

6. Extraterrestrial __ __ __ __ __

7. To begin __ __ __ __ __

8. Water that falls from the sky __ __ __ __

Art by Allison Black

SNAIL SHOPPING

Xu's favorite pet store is a little unusual. Two elevators stop only on certain floors, and the caterpillars keep escaping from their habitat. Find the 15 caterpillars. Then figure out how many times Xu had to change elevators to complete his to-do list in order.

Xu's To-Do's

1. Buy pet snail.

2. Have snail groomed.

3. Go to gastropod obedience class.

4. Buy *Snail Without Fail* book.

5. Grab a seaweed-mushroom smoothie.

6. Take photo with new friend!

WORDS AND OBJECTS

While some pooches play, the others are hard at work! There are 8 WORDS hidden on this page that match the 8 OBJECTS hidden on the next page. Can you find them all?

Keep track of the names of the objects you find in the spaces below.

_ _ _ _ _ _ _ _   _ _ _ _ _ _ _

_ _ _ _ _ _   _ _ _ _ _

_ _ _ _ _ _ _ _ _ _ _   _ _ _ _ _ _ _

_ _ _ _ _ _   _ _ _ _ _

Art by Howard McWilliam

99

SPIDER WEB

Spencer the spider got home from a long day at the silk factory. Help him find his way through the spider web maze to get to his bed.

START

FINISH

Art by Luisa Uribe

MUSTACHE MEMORY

Quick! Study this page for 60 seconds. Then go to the top of the next page to test your memory. Be on the lookout for a hidden puzzle piece!

Art by Brian White

TEST YOUR MEMORY

Did you study the scene on the previous page? Now see if you can answer these questions. Circle your responses. No peeking!

1 How many creatures are competing in the mustache contest?

1   3   4

2 What is the little fish next to the judge doing?

EATING A SNACK   LOOKING AT HIS PHONE   WRITING NOTES

3 What is the correct color of the judge's hair?

4 Which of these does NOT appear in the picture?

A BOW TIE   A STARFISH   AN OCTOPUS

5 Where is the hidden puzzle piece?

ON THE JUDGE'S VEST   ON THE GREEN FISH   ON THE SIGN

POPPY'S COPIES

Poppy Okapi had a sale at her photocopy business. Copies cost 10 cents per sheet of paper. How much did each of today's customers pay?

1. Myna Byrd made **33** copies of her short poem "Byrds of a Feather" to give to friends.

2. Don Key made **40** copies of a flyer for the community-theater production of *Home of the Bray*.

3. Al Paca made **2** dozen copies of his flyer for the annual neighborhood yard sale.

4. Bob Catt made **3** copies of his 16-page book *Catt Tales*.

Art by Pat Lewis

KITTY CITY

There's an impostor hiding in this clowder of cats. It's furry, it barks, and it wags its tail when excited. Can you find it in the picture?

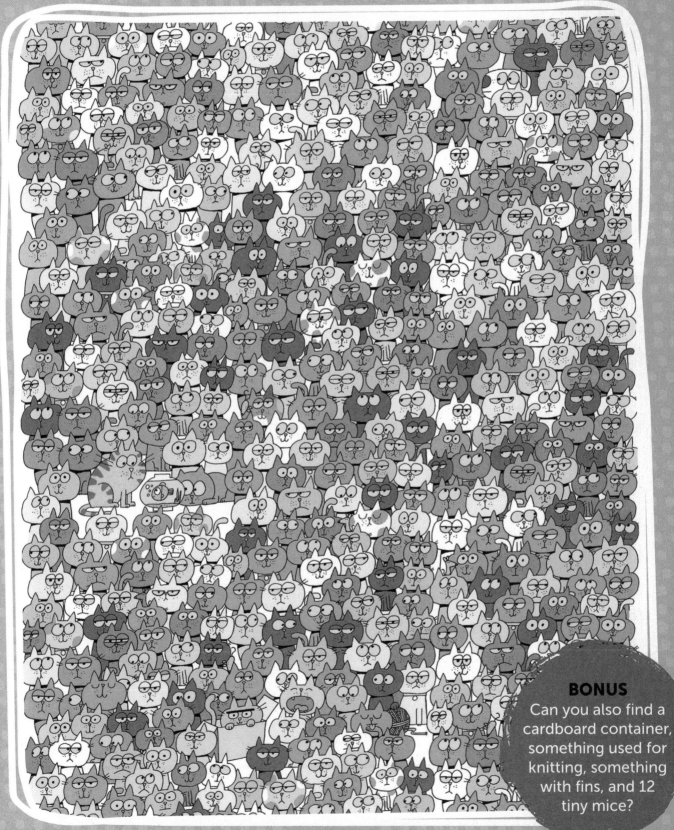

Art by Travis Foster

BONUS
Can you also find a cardboard container, something used for knitting, something with fins, and 12 tiny mice?

LONG-JUMP LEAPERS

This event is really hopping! First use the secret code to figure out what objects are hidden in the scene. Then use the list to find the 20 hidden objects in the big picture.

CODE CRACKER

Each letter in the code is the letter in the alphabet that comes after the real letter. So, for example, a B in the code would signify that the letter is really an A. And the code word DBU would stand for CAT.

1 C P P L

2 Q B S U Z   I B U

3 V N C S F M M B

4 D P N C

5 T M J D F   P G   D B L F

6 D B O P F

7 C S P D D P M J

8 C P P N F S B O H

9 D V Q D B L F

10 Q J D L B Y

11 T B V D F Q B O

12 E P N J O P

13 N V T J D B M   O P U F

14 G J T I

15 C B O B O B

16 I F B S U

17 U P P U I C S V T I

18 T O B L F

19 Q F O D J M

20 G J T I I P P L

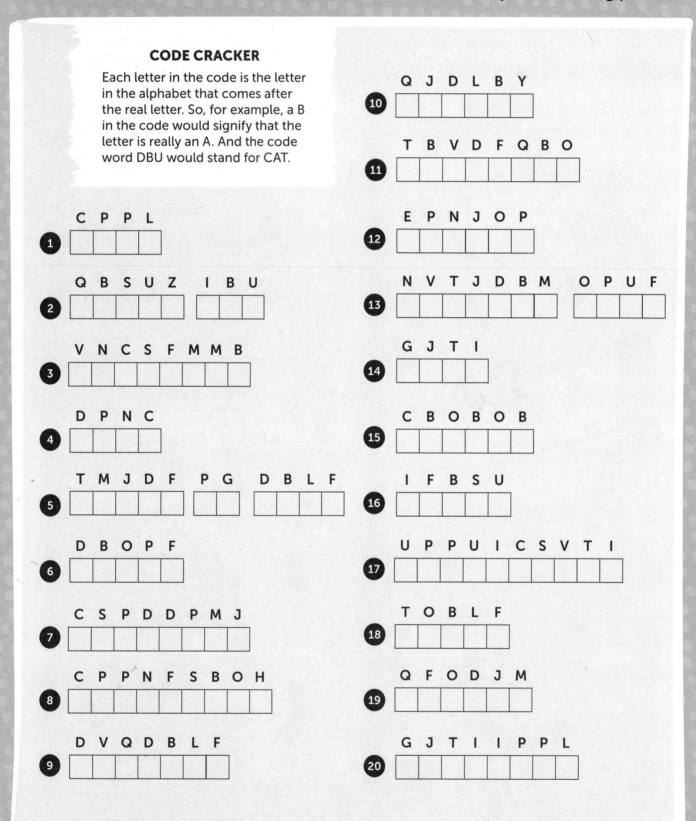

104

GO, TEAM CRISSCROSS!

It's game time! These 35 words about sports fit together in the grid in only one way. Use the number of letters in each word as a clue to where the word might fit. We started you off with BALL.

WORD LIST

3 LETTERS

BAT
RUN
TIE
WIN

4 LETTERS

~~BALL~~
FANS
GAME
GOAL
JUMP
LOSE
TEAM

5 LETTERS

CATCH
COURT
FIELD
GLOVE
SCORE

6 LETTERS

CHEERS
POINTS
SOCCER
TROPHY
UMPIRE

7 LETTERS

JERSEYS
REFEREE

8 LETTERS

BASEBALL
FOOTBALL
HALFTIME
PRACTICE
SOFTBALL
TRAINING

9 LETTERS

TEAMMATES

10 LETTERS

BASKETBALL
SCOREBOARD
TOURNAMENT

12 LETTERS

CHAMPIONSHIP

AW, NUTS!

Can you find the 22 canoes hiding
in this pile of pistachios?

READY, SET, GO!

In this scene, 10 items have been replaced by a rhyming item. For example, a seat has been replaced by a beet. How many others can you find?

BONUS
Find 8 things that rhyme with *go*.

Art by Pat Lewis

FIND THOSE FISH

There are 14 tropical fish swimming through these grids. Using the directions and hints below, can you figure out where all the fish go?

Look at the grids. Each numbered square tells you how many of the empty squares touching it (above, below, left, right, or diagonally) contain a fish. Write an X on squares that can't have a fish. Then write an F on squares that have a fish.

Photos by Inusuke/iStock (fish in coral); Burnsboxco/iStock (other fish)

HINTS:

- A fish cannot go in a square that has a number.

- Put an X on all the squares touching a zero.

- Even if you're not sure where to put all the fish connected to a number, fill in the ones you are sure of.

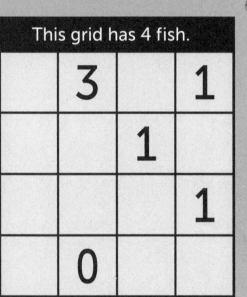

This grid has 4 fish.

	3		1
		1	
			1
	0		

This grid has 10 fish.

			2		
	0				2
		1	4		
	3				
			1		3
3					

SUPER CHALLENGE!

Try not to get crabby as you wait in line for the seashell open house. Without clues or knowing what to look for, see if you can find all 24 hidden objects before the event starts.

Art by Daryll Collins

ROAD TRIP!

Try not to get crabby as you wait in line for the seashell open house. Without clues or knowing what to look for, see if you can find all 24 hidden objects before the event starts.

START

When you tour the capital of Washington, where are you?

Olympia   Seattle

You take a trip down the entire Mississippi River. Where do you first board your boat?

Minnesota

South Dakota

If you visit the coast of California, which ocean splashes you?

Atlantic   Pacific

From the southern border of Utah, which state can you see?

Arizona   Montana

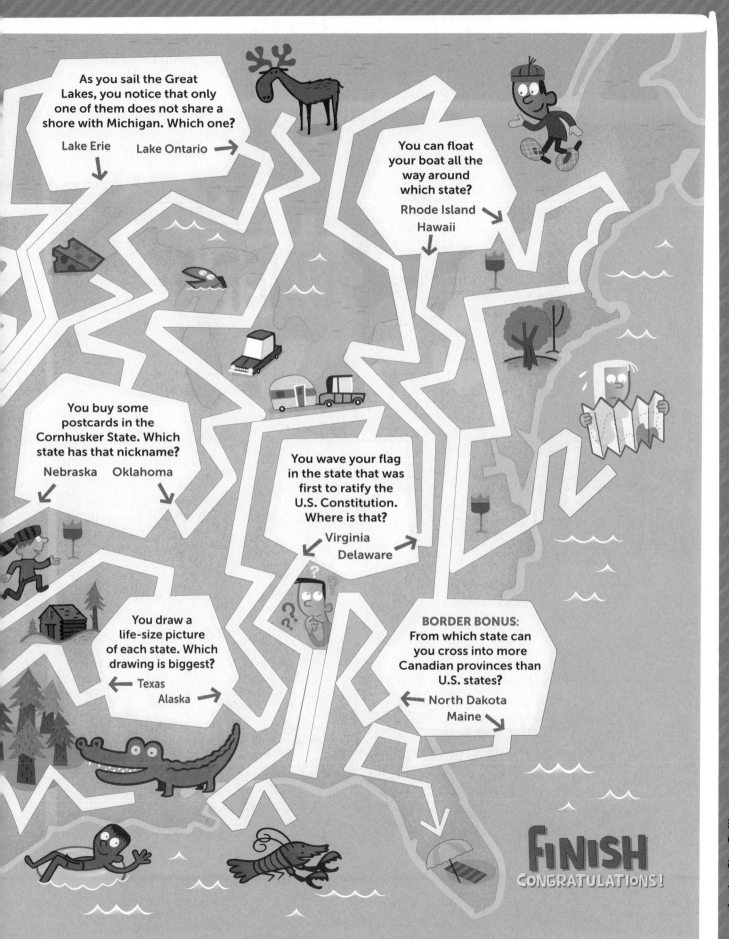

As you sail the Great Lakes, you notice that only one of them does not share a shore with Michigan. Which one?

Lake Erie

Lake Ontario →

You can float your boat all the way around which state?

Rhode Island →

Hawaii

You buy some postcards in the Cornhusker State. Which state has that nickname?

Nebraska

Oklahoma

You wave your flag in the state that was first to ratify the U.S. Constitution. Where is that?

Virginia

Delaware →

You draw a life-size picture of each state. Which drawing is biggest?

← Texas

Alaska →

BORDER BONUS:
From which state can you cross into more Canadian provinces than U.S. states?

← North Dakota

Maine →

FINISH
CONGRATULATIONS!

DINER DOUBLE

How many pairs of matching sea creatures can you find?

BIRDS OF A FEATHER

Find each pattern below in the grid.

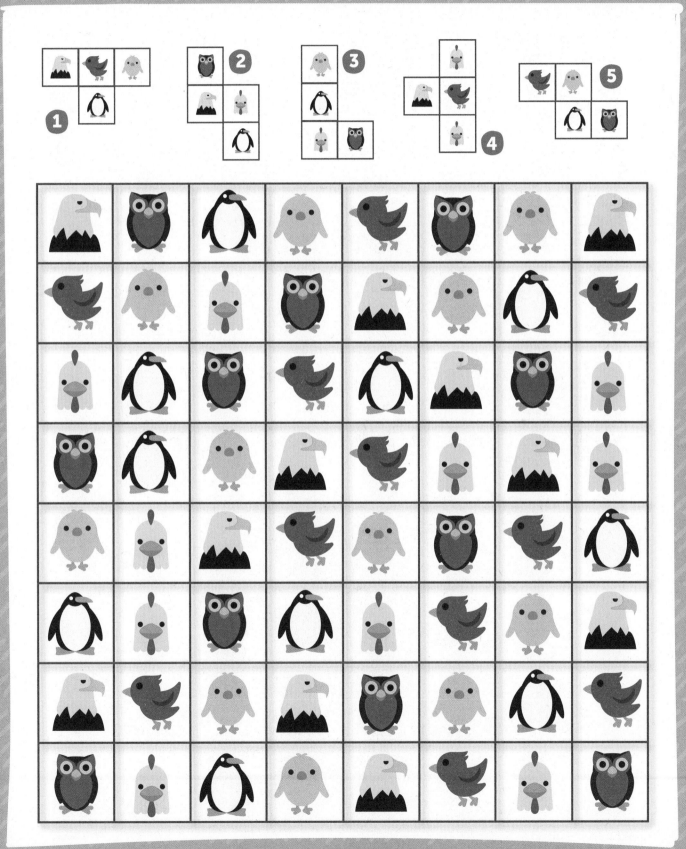

BACK TO SCHOOL

Can you find 8 basketballs, 8 number eights, 5 pencils, 5 skateboards, 8 water bottles, 6 smiley faces, 3 globes, and 3 zebras?

Art by Nathan Daniels

ANIMAL SQUARES

The animals have gotten all mixed up at the fair. Following the rules below, can you find nine animal names in the box? The first one has been done for you.

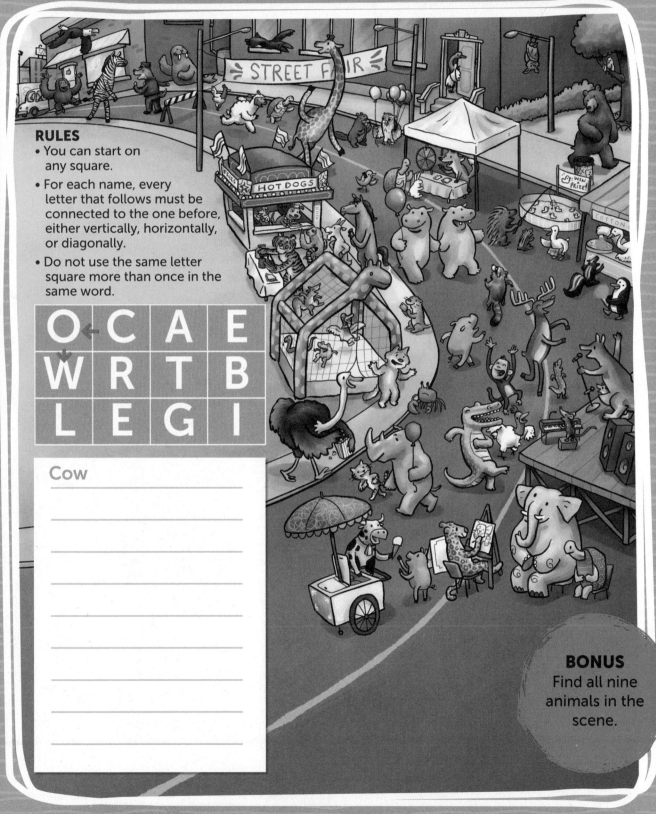

RULES

- You can start on any square.
- For each name, every letter that follows must be connected to the one before, either vertically, horizontally, or diagonally.
- Do not use the same letter square more than once in the same word.

O	C	A	E
W	R	T	B
L	E	G	I

Cow

BONUS
Find all nine animals in the scene.

Each of these small scenes contains 6 hidden objects from the list below. Some objects are hidden in more than one scene. Can you find the 6 hidden objects in each scene?

HIDDEN OBJECT LIST

artist's brush (4)
banana (3)
button (3)
crescent moon (3)
drinking straw (3)
envelope (4)
fish (2)
pencil (3)
ring (3)
sock (2)
toothbrush (3)
yo-yo (2)

BONUS
Two scenes contain the exact same set of hidden objects. Can you find that matching pair?

The numbers tell you how many times each object is hidden.

Art by Iryna Bodnaruk

121

CROSSWORD VACATION

Fill in the correct answers then start packing your bags! If you don't know the answer to a clue, look at the other clues that are around it, both across and down, or try another part of the puzzle and come back to the tough clue later.

ACROSS

1 Commercials

4 Fog; rhymes with *daze*

8 Signal from a ship in trouble

11 "Skip to My ____, My Darlin' "

12 You screw this onto a jar (2 words)

13 Fuzz in one's belly button or in the dryer

14 Summer vacation activity in a pool, a lake, or an ocean

16 China's continent

17 "Hold ____ ____your hat!" (2 words)

18 Summer vacation activity with a tent

20 How chic!: "____ la la!"

23 Rodent in a lab

24 Cloth for cleaning; rhymes with *tag*

27 Religious woman who lives in a convent

29 Outfits worn by the ancient Romans

33 Place with rides that you visit during summer vacation (2 words)

36 Another word for *mothers*

37 One of five on your foot

38 Messy place a pig calls home

39 ____ Willie Winkie

41 They perform checkups (abbreviation)

43 Vacation transportation (two-wheeled)

47 "____ upon a time . . ."

51 Not busy; rhymes with *bridle*

52 Summer vacation activity that you play with a bat

55 Close-by

56 Kitchen appliance you use for baking

57 Negative answers; opposite of *yeses*

58 What beavers build

59 Unwanted plant in a garden

60 Our closest primate

DOWN

1 "One more thing . . ."

2 One of two directions in a crossword puzzle

3 Business outfit

4 *Green Eggs and ____*

5 ____ *Baba and the Forty Thieves*

6 ____ oxide (sunscreen compound)

7 Mystery writer ____ Allan Poe

8 "Yes, yes" in Spanish (2 words)

9 "The door's open. Come ____ ____!" (2 words)

10 Male deer

13 Portable computer

15 Cow's sound

19 "Never mind. It doesn't ____ ."

21 "I'll be there in ____ ____." (immediately; 2 words)

22 Low, buzzing sound; rhymes with *gum*

24 Male sheep

25 I ____ ____ child (2 words)

26 Bubble ____

28 Hit the tennis ball over the ____

30 "Food" for cars

31 Drawing or painting class

32 Cloud's home

34 *Tom* ____ (Mark Twain novel; rhymes with *lawyer*)

35 Head movement for a yes response

40 Bendable part of the arm

42 Cry uncontrollably

43 In a ____ (stuck)

44 A thought

45 Seafood often served in chowder

46 Roof overhang

48 Nickname for grandma

49 Sound of a hoof on pavement: clip ____

50 "Would you like anything ____ ?"

53 Look at; observe

54 Finish

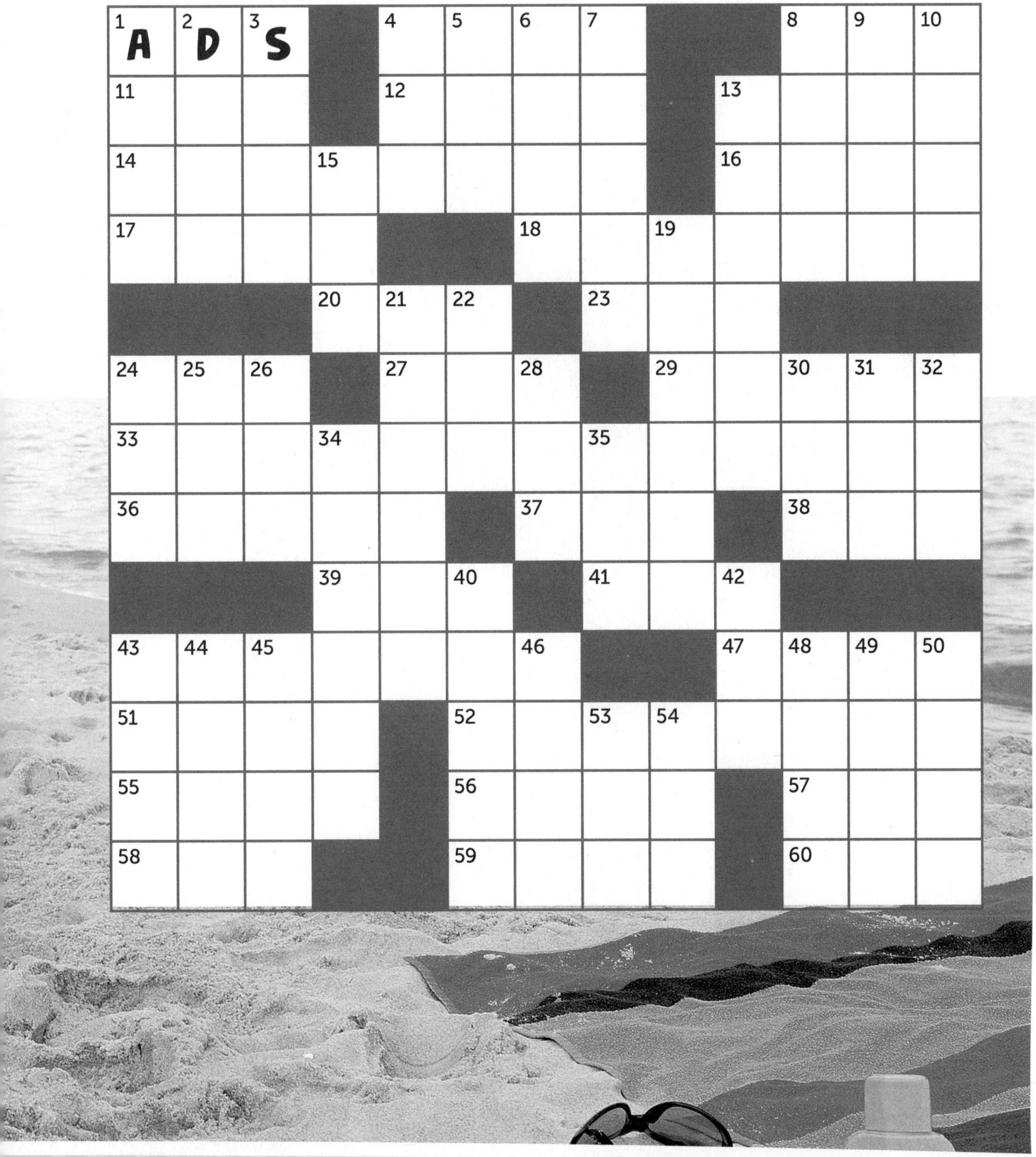

Photos by Image Source/Superstock

PAJAMA DAY

Ms. Z's students really get into Pajama Day. No snoozing as you search for the 19 hidden objects in the classroom scene below.

Now look for 11 differences between the nearly identical scenes on these two pages.

Art by Kelly Kennedy

WHAT'S THE BUZZ?

We don't mean to bug you. But we would like you to search for the 35 insect names hiding in this grid. Look for them up, down, across, and diagonally. How many can you spot?

WORD LIST

APHID	HOUSEFLY
BEDBUG	KATYDID
BEETLE	LADYBUG
BLOWFLY	LEAFHOPPER
BUTTERFLY	LOCUST
CICADA	LOUSE
COCKROACH	MANTIS
CRICKET	MAYFLY
DRAGONFLY	MEALYBUG
EARWIG	MIDGE
FIRE ANT	MOSQUITO
FIREFLY	MOTH
FLEA	SILVERFISH
FRUIT FLY	STINKBUG
GNAT	TERMITE
GRASSHOPPER	WALKING STICK
HONEYBEE	WEEVIL
HORNET	

ENCHANTED FOREST MAZE

Find a path from START to FINISH. Then find the woodpecker, rabbit, fairy, and squirrel.

FINISH

START

Art by Matt Lyon

T E F R U I T F L Y Y L F E R I F
E E B U Z Z T S I L V E R F I S H
R B M N E T M E A L Y B U G O X K
M Y N Y S A L J N C R I C K E T L
I E U U U C O C K R O A C H F G E
T N C L O D D R A G O N F L Y U A F
E O F Y L F W O L B R H K P G B F
L H B G U B K N I T S V A H K Y H
E B E D B U G X A W Y U T O W D O
K L Y M B U T T E R F L Y U H A P
M A Y F L Y A V L S R X D S I L P
P D R O N E N V F M X V I E R E E
W A L K I N G S T I C K D F R O R
E W E E V I L E A N V I J L U T S
C A P H E E L G H C M S C Y G P I
H P R C V T D T O F I R E A N T T
I H X W E V O E G D I M D U D V N
R I T E I M O S Q U I T O H N A A
P D B Y P G R A S S H O P P E R M

BONUS:

Unscramble the letters to learn an insect's favorite sport.

R C K I E T C.

Unscramble the letters to find a veggie bugs hate.

Q S A S U H.

Art by Carolina Farias

WORDS AND OBJECTS

What a beautiful day for a bike ride! There are 8 WORDS hidden on this page that match the 8 OBJECTS hidden on the next page. Can you find them all?

Art by Iryna Bodnaruk

128

130

SOCCER MEMORY

Quick! Study this page for 60 seconds. Then go to the top of the next page to test your memory. Be on the lookout for a hidden puzzle piece!

Art by Brian Michael Weaver

TEST YOUR MEMORY

Did you study the scene on the previous page? Now see if you can answer these questions. Circle your responses. No peeking!

1 What color are the ants on the field?

2 How many ants are actually playing on the field?   8   10   9

3 Which of these is one of the signs in the stands:

GO ANTS!   SCORE!   HOORAY FOR ANTS!

4 Which of these insects is NOT on the sidelines?

BUTTERFLY   BUMBLEBEE   LADYBUG

5 Where is the hidden puzzle piece?

IN THE STANDS   ON THE WALL   IN THE GRASS

AT THE MOVIES

Each movie theater snack costs a different dollar amount. The totals for all four snacks across each row and down each column are noted. It's up to you to find the cost of each snack. Popcorn is $8.00. Start with the bottom row.

$17.00
$28.00
$20.00
$26.00

$24.00 $22.00 $23.00 $22.00

🍿 = $8.00   🍭 = _____
🥨 = _____   ▨ = _____
                  🍦 = _____

132

FROG FRENZY

There's an impostor hiding in this army of frogs. It's a reptile with a shell. Can you find it in the picture?

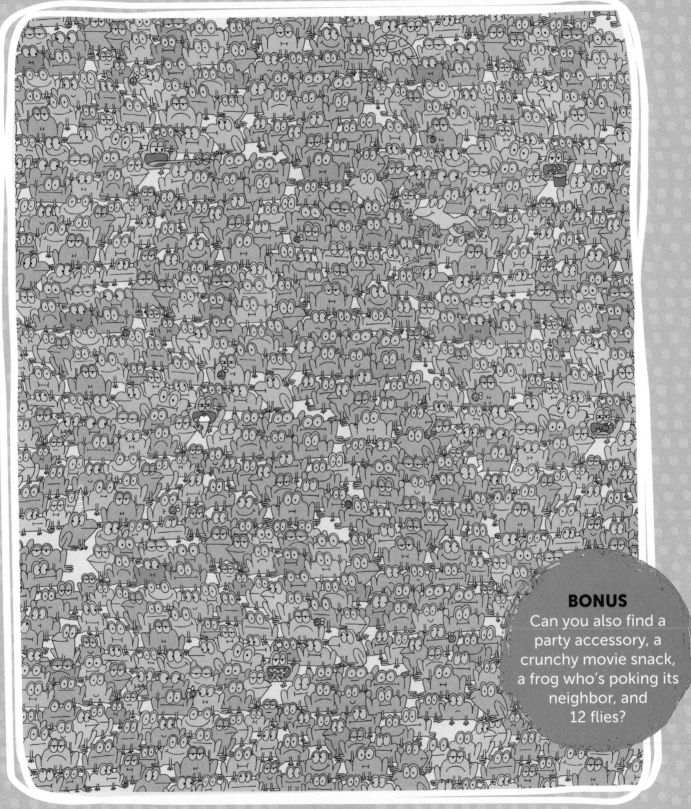

Art by Travis Foster

BONUS
Can you also find a party accessory, a crunchy movie snack, a frog who's poking its neighbor, and 12 flies?

RAINY DAY ON THE FARM

These farm animals are staying cozy during the storm. First use the clues below to figure out the words. Each word is a hidden object to find in the big scene. Once you've found the 14 hidden objects, transfer the letters with numbers into the correct spaces on the next page to learn the answer to the riddle.

1 It floats and has a mast.

__ __ __ __ __ __ __
               8

2 A handheld tool you twist to tighten metal fasteners

__ __ __ __ __ __ __ __ __ __
   9   14

3 A hard piece of candy on a stick

__ __ __ __ __ __ __ __
         12

4 Wear one on your foot to stay dry in rain or snow.

__ __ __ __
  2

5 You might eat one with syrup for breakfast.

__ __ __ __ __ __
       10

6 You can paddle down a stream in one.

__ __ __ __ __
  15

7 It may change color and fall from a tree in autumn.

__ __ __ __
  5

8 Use this to slap a puck into a goal.

__ __ __ __ __ __ __ __ __
    1   16

9 A tool used to make watercolor paintings

__ __ __ __ __ __
13   11
__ __ __ __ __
  3

10 It protects your hand from hot pots and pans.

__ __ __ __ __ __ __ __

11 You may hit a homerun with this.

__ __ __ __ __ __ __
    18
__ __ __
  6

12 Use this portable device to see during a power outage.

__ __ __ __ __ __ __ __ __ __
      19

13 Throw this toy and it will come back to you.

__ __ __ __ __ __ __ __ __
    7   4

14 You can use it to flip your pancakes.

__ __ __ __ __ __ __
     17

Art by Brian Michael Weaver

Why is it better to eat doughnuts in the rain?

— — — — — — — — — — — — — — — — — —
1 2 3   4 5 6   7 8 9 10   11 12 13 14 15 16 17 18 19

COUNTDOWN TO LAUNCH

These 41 space terms fit together in the grid in only one way. Use the number of letters in each word as a clue to where it might fit. We started you off with ROCKET. Once you fill everything in, unscramble the highlighted letters to find the answer to the riddle.

4 LETTERS

CREW

FUEL

MOON

TEST

5 LETTERS

EAGLE

EARTH

ORBIT

SOYUZ

SPACE

6 LETTERS

APOLLO

CLOUDS

GEMINI

LAUNCH

METEOR

OXYGEN

PLANET

ROCKET

SKYLAB

STAGES

STARRY

STRAIN

7 LETTERS

AIRLOCK

CONTROL

DOCKING

ECLIPSE

GRAVITY

MERCURY

MISSION

SHUTTLE

8 LETTERS

BLAST OFF

9 LETTERS

ASTEROIDS

ASTRONAUT

ASTRONOMY

DISCOVERY

HALF-LIGHT

SATELLITE

SPACEWALK

10 LETTERS

ATMOSPHERE

EXPEDITION

SPACECRAFT

TRAJECTORY

ROCKET

Why did the astronaut smile during takeoff?

___ ___ ____ __ _____

JELLY JAMBOREE

Can you pick out the 22 balloons hiding among these jellyfish?

RIDDLE SUDOKU

Fill in the squares so the six letters appear only once in each row, column, and 2 × 3 box. Then read the highlighted squares to find the answer to each riddle.

Our Sudoku puzzles use letters instead of numbers.

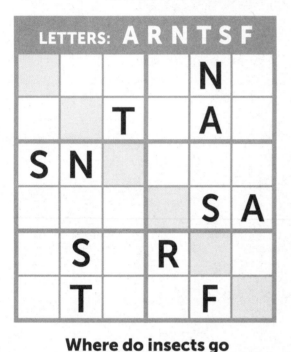

LETTERS: A R N T S F

				N	
		T		A	
S	N				
			S	A	
	S		R		
	T			F	

Where do insects go on vacation?

ANSWER:___ __ __ __ __ __.

LETTERS: D P E R Y S

					P
E			R		S
D			P	R	
	E	P			Y
P		S			D
			S		

What do you call an undercover arachnid?

ANSWER: A __ __ __ __ __ __.

CREEPY-CRAWLY CALCULATIONS

To solve the riddle, use the fractions of the words below.
The first one has been done for you.

What did the itchy dog say to the flea?

1. Last ⅓ of LOCUST
2. Last ⅛ of MOSQUITO
3. Last ¼ of WASP

4. Last ½ of BEDBUG
5. Last ⅙ of EARWIG
6. First ¼ of INCHWORM

7. Last ¼ of SLUG
8. First ⅙ of MANTIS
9. Last ⅓ of BEE

S T __ __ __ __ __ __ __ __ __ __ __!

SHADOW MATCH

Take a look at the shadows and match each one to a tasty frozen treat below.

BIG DINOSAUR DIG

Chip your way from START to FINISH by answering each question correctly. You'll have to dig deep into your dinosaur knowledge, no bones about it.

START

Horns Aplenty
How do scientists think *Triceratops* used its horns?

To carry food and drink trays at parties

To battle with other *Triceratops*, the way rhinoceroses do today

Dinosaur Clues
How do we know about dinosaurs?

From their classic TV shows, like *I Love Lucianovenator*

From their fossils, such as bones, skin and feather imprints, and poop

Mega Mom
Why is *Maiasaura* called the "good mother lizard"?

Its arm bones were curved for cradling infants.

Its fossils were found with nests of its eggs and babies.

Everyday Dinos
Some dinosaurs did not go extinct. Which animals are living dinosaurs?

Birds

Alligators and crocodiles

Saurus Squad
Why do scientists think some plant-eating dinosaurs moved in herds?

Those dinosaurs were chatty and loved company.

Fossilized trackways show many of them walking in the same direction.

SUPER CHALLENGE!

There is a celebration tonight on the island of Molokai. Without clues or knowing what to look for, can you find the 28 hidden objects in the scene?

STARGAZING

There are 14 stars shining in these grids. Using the directions and hints below, can you figure out where all the stars go?

Look at the grids. Each numbered square tells you how many of the empty squares touching it (above, below, left, right, or diagonally) contain a star. Write an X on squares that can't have a star. Then write an S on squares that have a star.

HINTS:

- A star cannot go in a square that has a number.

- Even if you're not sure where to put all the stars around a number, fill in the ones you are sure of.

- Keep trying possibilities with a pencil and eraser!

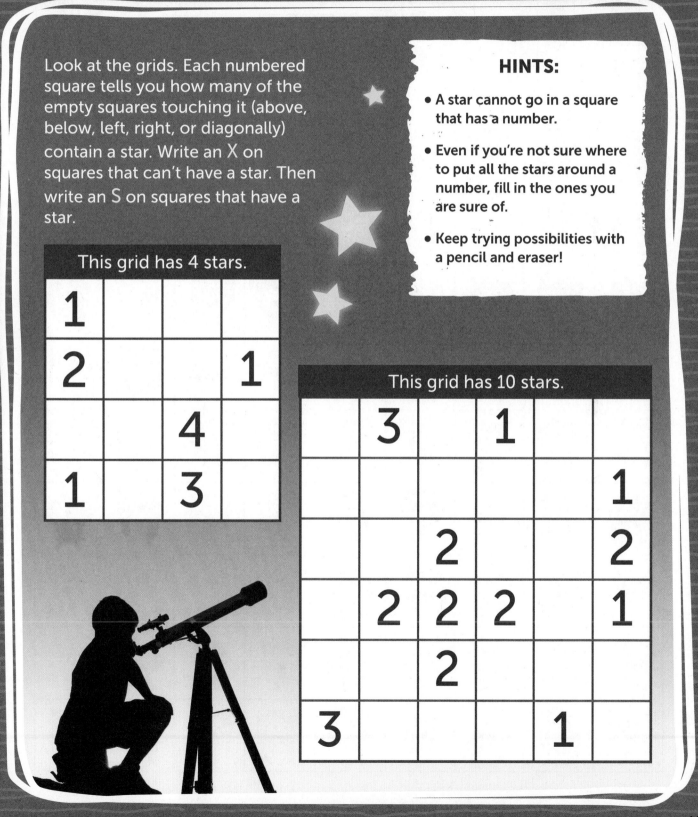

This grid has 4 stars.

1			
2			1
		4	
1		3	

This grid has 10 stars.

	3		1	
				1
		2		2
	2	2	2		1
		2		
3				1

MONSTER MATCH

Find each pattern below in the grid.

NUMBER HOUSE

The Numberman family loves numbers! Can you find one 1, two 2s, three 3s, four 4s, five 5s, six 6s, seven 7s, eight 8s, and nine 9s hidden in the scene?

Each of these small scenes contains 6 hidden objects from the list below. Some objects are hidden in more than one scene. Can you find the 6 hidden objects in each scene?

HIDDEN OBJECT LIST

baseball (2)
cane (4)
crescent moon (4)
fish (3)
fried egg (2)
heart (4)
mitten (2)
mug (3)
ruler (3)
slice of bread (3)
slice of cake (3)
tack (3)

BONUS
Two scenes contain the exact same set of hidden objects. Can you find that matching pair?

The numbers tell you how many times each object is hidden.

Art by Jannie Ho

149

GOING IN CIRCLES

Go around and around using the clues to fill in the spaces. The last letter of each word will also be the first letter of the next word.

1. Hot-fudge dessert
6. Opposite of full
10. The yellow of an egg
13. A baby cat
18. Short time of sleep
20. A "pie" with cheese
24. Similar to a crocodile
32. "_____ and shine!"
35. Our home planet
39. Pumps oxygen to the body
20. Big brass instrument
46. Not multiplication, division, or subtraction
53. Five cents
58. A large spotted cat
64. A double-_____ bus
69. Smallest state in the U.S.
79. Rumba, salsa, or tap
83. Opposite of begin
85. Snare or bass
88. St. Patrick's Day month
92. Sport with a puck
97. Japanese money
99. Direction a compass points
103. A kind of crab
107. Things you floss
112. Opposite of good-bye

How many
sides does a
circle have?

Two—the inside
and the outside.

Art by Jim Steck

PARADE DAY

People in New Orleans have come out to celebrate Mardi Gras. Before the parade is over, see if you can find all 19 hidden objects in the scene below.

Now look for 8 differences between the nearly identical scenes on these two pages.

Art by Mary Sullivan

GO WITH THE FLOW

There are at least 19 objects, words, and actions at this campsite that rhyme with GO, including six that have more than one syllable. Can you find them all?

Art by Jessixa Bagley

155

WORDS AND OBJECTS

There are 8 WORDS hidden on this page that match the 8 OBJECTS hidden on the next page. Can you find them all?

Keep track of the names of the objects you find in the spaces below.

— — — — — — — — — —
— — — — — — — — — —
— — — — — — — — — — — — — — —
— — — — — — — — — — — — — — — — —

RAIN OR SHINE

START

To go from this maze's cloudy START to its sunny FINISH, you have to find the one path that takes you through alternating clouds and suns. You may not retrace or cross your path.

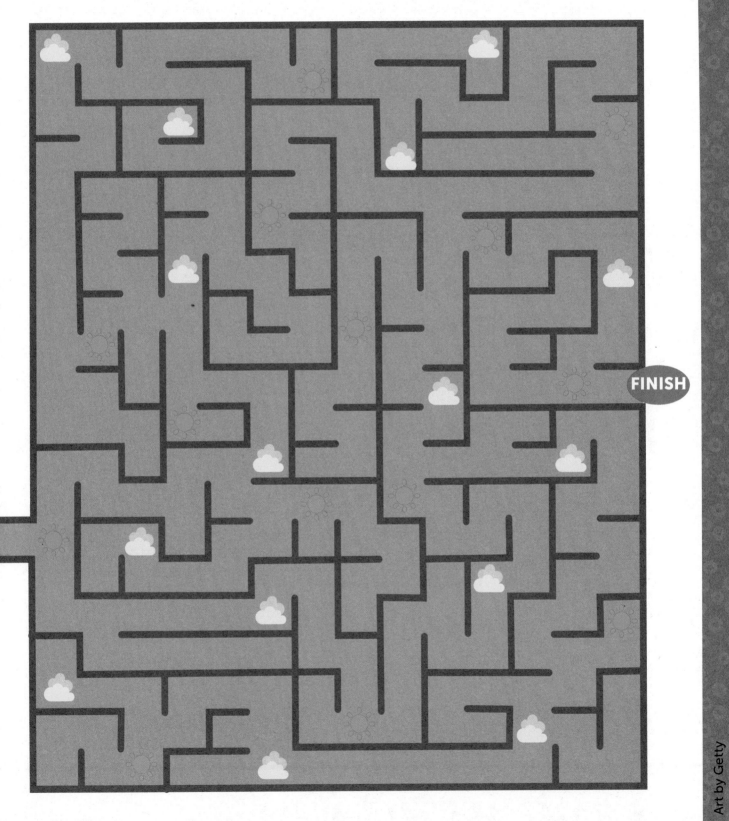

FINISH

159

RUNNING ERRANDS

Catrick has a busy day ahead. He wrote down his errands in the order he plans to do them. If he starts from his house, how many times will he cross the bridge?

DOG WASH MEMORY

Quick! Study this page for 60 seconds. Then go to the top of the next page to test your memory. Be on the lookout for a hidden puzzle piece!

Art by James Yamasaki

TEST YOUR MEMORY

Did you study the scene on the previous page? Now see if you can answer these questions. Circle your responses. No peeking!

1 How many people are in the scene?   7   9   11

2 What is the boy in the front holding in his hand?

A BASEBALL   A BAR OF SOAP   A SPONGE

3 What is the correct color of the bucket?

4 Which one of these is NOT in the scene?

A TOWEL   A CAR   A HOSE

5 Where is the hidden puzzle piece?

ON A SHIRT   IN A TREE   IN A PUDDLE

TAKE IT OR LEAF IT

Start at each blank leaf and follow its branch to the trunk.
Can you find:

1. The branch that has only odd-numbered leaves?

2. The branch with leaves that add up to exactly 19?

3. The branch with leaves that add up to the highest score of any branch?

4. The branch with leaves that add up to the lowest score?

BUNCH OF BUNNIES

There's an impostor hiding in this fluffle of bunnies. It likes acorns, has a bushy tail, and sleeps underground or in trees. Can you find it in the picture?

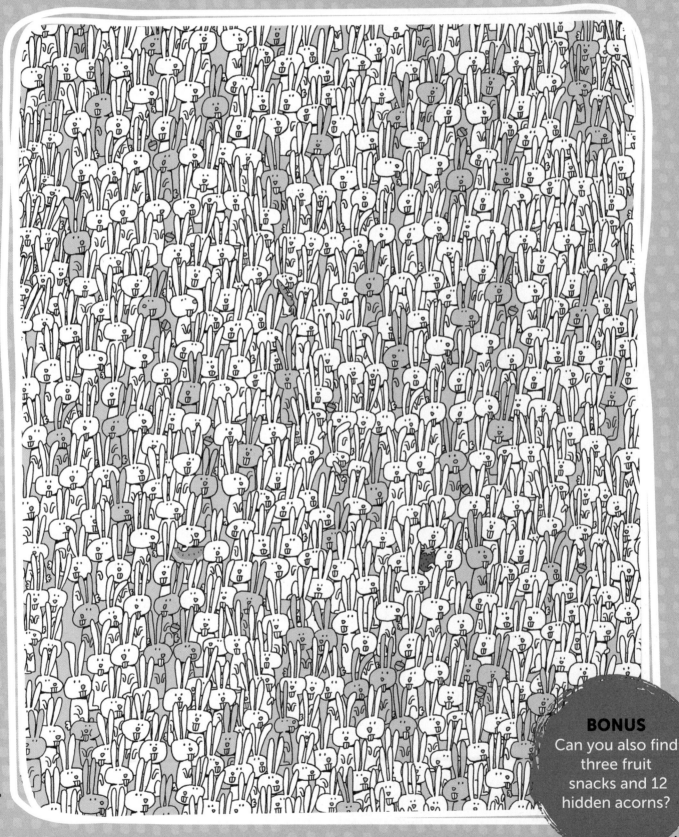

Art by Travis Foster

BONUS
Can you also find three fruit snacks and 12 hidden acorns?

THE FEATHER CHANNEL

ABC (All-Bird Cable) is showing a documentary on humans. To join the fun, first use the secret code to figure out what objects are hidden in the scene. Then use the list to find the 16 hidden objects in the big picture.

CODE CRACKER

To discover the objects, write down only the capital letters. So, for example, "xoyeCsadoUsdeP" is "CUP."

1 aBxdiEadmxLadL

_____ BELL

2 FaedIxxdfSoweHe

_____ FISH

3 vvaKswoIjuTaahsEah

_____ KITE

4 yurTiAponxCoeKoe

_____ TACK

5 weYqwhOne-sYkaO

_____ - _____ YO-YO

6 kCrtyANwsdOpiEaa

_____ CANOE

7 oiRkpcUmnLwaEiopR

_____ RULER

8 SyuCwepAnjRbnwFro

_____ SCARF

9 BoimAhhgNerANtyrAs

_____ BANANA

10 yuBeeAoSpiEniBryiAnLpLe

_____ BASEBALL

11 EuiNhsVicEmtLObmPxzE

_____ ENVELOPE

12 pmFIgerxSaHHnbaOyOnK

_____ FISHHOOK

13 evAyRvsTInSxTwo'Sc dBesRUxiwScxH

_____ _____ ARTIST'S BRUSH

14 pCbhREwSiuCEmvNTi uMpzOhOiuN

_____ CRESCENT MOON

15 SLuhInrCEn qOgFn bPxxIumZuZhA

_____ SLICE OF PIZZA

16 abDReoIsNqtKvbINooGa beSaTieRobxAsnWo

_____ DRINKING STRAW

FELINE FRIENDS

The 28 kinds of cats listed here fit into the grid in just one way. Find the *purr*-fect spot for each one!

WORD LIST

4 LETTERS

MANX

5 LETTERS

KORAT

6 LETTERS

BENGAL

BIRMAN

BOMBAY

EXOTIC

OCICAT

SOMALI

SPHYNX

7 LETTERS

CHAUSIE

PERSIAN

RAGDOLL

8 LETTERS

BALINESE

DEVON REX

SIBERIAN

SNOWSHOE

9 LETTERS

CHARTREUX

MAINE COON

PETERBALD

SINGAPURA

TONKINESE

10 LETTERS

ABYSSINIAN

CORNISH REX

HIGHLANDER

TURKISH VAN

11 LETTERS

RUSSIAN BLUE

12 LETTERS

SCOTTISH FOLD

15 LETTERS

NORWEGIAN
FOREST

TEEING UP

There are 25 golf tees hiding in this frigid scene. Can you find them all?

FOR ANSWERS

There are 29 different fish words and phrases hidden in this grid. For each one, the word FISH has been replaced by Look up, down, across, backwards, and diagonally.

WORD LIST

angelfish	flying fish
archerfish	goldfish
blowfish	jellyfish
bluefish	kingfish
bonefish	noodle fish
butterfish	parrot fish
catfish	ribbonfish
crayfish	scorpion fish
cuttlefish	shellfish
dogfish	starfish
fishbowl	sunfish
fisherman	swordfish
fish-eye	triggerfish
fishhook	zebra fish
fishtail	

B U T T E R 🐟 **G G O L D** 🐟
O L 🐟 **E L T T U C L D N D**
F I E P A R R O T 🐟 **O I R**
F A R C H E R 🐟 **S I** 🐟 **H O**
L T M H A I R C P H 🐟 **L W**
Y 🐟 **A V B E R R O E W** 🐟 **S**
I E N B G A O O N O T E U
N W O G Y C K O B E O U N
G N I 🐟 **S T B** 🐟 **Y E E L** 🐟
🐟 **R D O G** 🐟 **L E G N A B R**
T T B L O W 🐟 **Y L L E J A**
K I N G 🐟 **Z E B R A** 🐟 **H T**
S H E L L 🐟 **E L D O O N S**

TRIVIA QUESTION:

What do goldfish have in the back of their throat?

Put the uncircled letters in order on the blanks.

__ __ __ __ __ __ __   __ __ __ __   __ __ __

__ __ __ __ __ !

CHIP IN

There are 12 chocolate chips in these grids. Using the directions and hints below, can you figure out where all the chocolate chips go?

Look at the grids. Each numbered square tells you how many of the empty squares touching it (above, below, left, right, or diagonally) contain a chocolate chip. Write an X on squares that can't have a chocolate chip. Then write CC on squares that have a chocolate chip.

HINTS:

- Put an *X* on all the squares touching a zero.

- Look in the corners where a numbered square may make it more obvious where a chocolate chip is hiding.

- A chocolate chip cannot go in a square that has number.

This grid has 2 chocolate chips.

1			
			0
	1		
			1

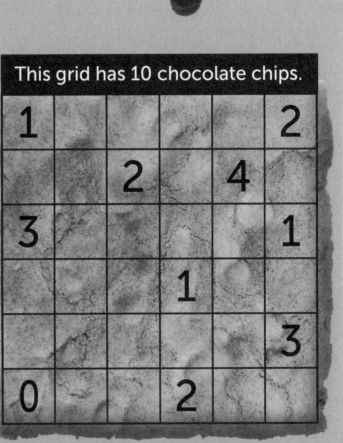

This grid has 10 chocolate chips.

1					2
		2		4	
3					1
			1		
					3
0			2		

172

FIND THAT FIDDLE

Each violin has an exact match—except one. Can you find it?

SUPER CHALLENGE!

The food in this space diner is out of this world! While you make up your mind what to order, see if you can find all 29 hidden objects in this scene.

artist's brush
banana
baseball
belt
candle
canoe
dog dish
envelope
eyeglasses
flashlight
football
glove
hockey stick
magnet
open umbrella
pennant
plunger
radish
ring
ruler
saw
seashell
skateboard
snail
sock
suitcase
tennis racket
toothbrush
wedge of lemon

JOIN THE BAND

Play your way from START to FINISH by answering each question correctly.

START

One Big Family

A typical concert band is made up of instruments in three categories, or families. They include

electric, acoustic, and voice.

woodwinds, brass, and percussion.

Metal Music

The ____ family is made up of instruments that usually have long, curved metal tubes, flared openings, cup-shaped mouthpieces, and valves or slides.

percussion

brass

What Wood You Call It?

A thin piece of wood-like material that is fastened over an instrument's mouthpiece and vibrates to make sound is called a

reed.

wood chip.

A Class on Brass

Which brass instrument is this?

Trombone

Trumpet

TOOT

Reed Aloud

Instruments that use reeds to make sound belong to the _____ family.

percussion

woodwind

Art by Dave Whamond

BEACH PATTERNS

Find each pattern below in the grid.

Art by Getty

ANIMAL STATION

In the scene below, can you find at least one thing that starts with each letter of the alphabet?

Art by Jennifer Harney

Each of these small scenes contains 6 hidden objects from the list below. Some objects are hidden in more than one scene. Can you find the 6 hidden objects in each scene?

HIDDEN OBJECT LIST

artist's brush (4)
baseball bat (4)
button (2)
crescent moon (3)
comb (4)
envelope (2)
glove (4)
key (2)
needle (3)
paper airplane (3)
pencil (2)
sock (3)

BONUS
Two scenes contain the exact same set of hidden objects. Can you find that matching pair?

The numbers tell you how many times each object is hidden.

Art by Iryna Bodnaruk

SEA HERE

The time has come to set sail and find your sea legs. There are 13 clues related to the sea in this puzzle. If you don't know the answer to a clue, look at the other clues that are around it, both across and down, or try another part of the puzzle and come back to the tough clue later.

ACROSS

1 Toward the back end of a boat

4 Yo-_____ (child's toy)

6 Lion zodiac sign

9 New England _____ chowder

11 Abbreviation for emergency room

12 Noah's boat

13 Write with a keyboard

14 Dives in the water with a mask, tank, and fins

16 Abbreviation for the city in CA where the movie business is

18 "School starts at 8 _____, not 8 PM."

19 Building that people sculpt on the beach

23 What a beach is made of

27 Pose a question

28 Means "and so on and so on" at the end of a list

30 Three, in Roman numerals

31 Classic beach toy

33 Lobsters grow and shed these

35 "_____, no! Here we go again!"

37 Tool used for chopping wood

38 "Apply _____ lotion with an SPF of at least 30"

42 "Who _____ _____?" Response to a knock (2 words)

46 "_____ we there yet?"

47 Opposite of yes

48 The rising and falling of the sea; high or low _____

49 An explosive

50 Abbreviation for doctor

51 Pro and _____

DOWN

1 Perform on the stage

2 Bug used as bait in fishing

3 Dance with metal-tipped shoes

4 Opposite of no

5 Killer whale

6 Where a scientist might work

7 Pitcher's stat

8 Gives the green light to

10 Ice cream does this if you leave it out

15 "Try to avoid *ers* and _____ during your speech."

17 Ginger _____ (soft drink)

19 Baseball player's hat

20 Neat _____ _____ pin (2 words)

21 A powerboat pulls you when you water-_____

22 Abbreviation for extraterrestrials

24 Come down with something; feel ill

25 Shutout in soccer

26 Slangy word for insult

29 Name of a dance, when the word is repeated three times

32 "Thanks a _____!"

34 "Follow the _____ signs to leave the building."

36 What you put a glove on

38 Fri., _____., Sun.

39 Large container for coffee, with a spigot

40 A fisherman might use this

41 Neither's partner

43 "_____ 'em, Fido!"

44 "_____ _____"; what brides and grooms say (2 words)

45 Total number of fingers

¹A	²F	³T		■	⁴	⁵	■	⁶	⁷	⁸
⁹			¹⁰	■	¹¹		■	¹²		
¹³				■	¹⁴		¹⁵			
■	■	■	¹⁶	¹⁷	■	¹⁸		■	■	■
¹⁹	²⁰	²¹			²²	■	²³	²⁴	²⁵	²⁶
²⁷			■	²⁸		²⁹	■	³⁰		
³¹			³²	■	³³		³⁴	■		
■	■	■	³⁵	³⁶	■	³⁷			■	■
³⁸	³⁹	⁴⁰			⁴¹	■	⁴²	⁴³	⁴⁴	⁴⁵
⁴⁶			■	⁴⁷		■	⁴⁸			
⁴⁹			■	⁵⁰		■	⁵¹			

DINO DANCE PARTY

This party sure is hopping! While these dancers show off their best moves, see if you can find all 17 hidden objects in the scene below.

Now look for 6 differences between the nearly identical scenes on these two pages.

RIDDLE SUDOKU

Our Sudoku puzzles use letters instead of numbers.

Fill in the squares so the six letters appear only once in each row, column, and 2 × 3 box. Then read the highlighted squares to find the answer to each riddle.

LETTERS: A C E H S W

	W		S	A	
S			E		
H			W		
		A			
		W			S
E	S	C		H	

What did the nut say when it sneezed?

ANSWER: __ __ __ __ __ __!

LETTERS: B I M R T U

		U	I		M
T					
	R		T		
		T		U	
					U
M		I	R		

What did the frog say when he saw the bunny?

ANSWER: __ __ __ __ __ __.

FAMILY HIKE

Each sentence below contains an item the Hale family took on their hike. Can you find them all? Hint: All the items are in the scene. **EXAMPLE:** Like all good hikers, we left the trail **unch**anged. (lunch)

1. Emma planned the route.
2. We stopped to sketch at the bridge.
3. Two squirrels came racing along a log!
4. The whole crew ate raisins for energy.
5. We came upon chopped trees near a beaver dam.
6. Our pace had to slow at challenging, rocky parts of the trail.

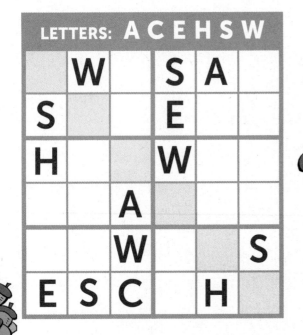

Kelly Kennedy (squirrel and acorns); Luke Flowers (hiking)

PASTA-TIVELY PERPLEXING

Rita Ravioli, Zoey Ziti, Terry Tortellini, and Marty Macaroni are the owners of the four businesses on Pasta Plaza. Use your noodle to figure out who owns each business.

CLUES

Terry either sells candy or grooms pets.

Rita's business is directly next to Terry's business.

Marty does not own the spa or the candy shop.

Zoey does not work in or directly next to the candy shop.

BONUS How many pieces of pasta can you find in the scene?

Art by Brian Michael Weaver

WORDS AND OBJECTS

Welcome to the International Yo-Yo Championships! There are 8 WORDS hidden on this page that match the 8 OBJECTS hidden on the next page. Can you find them all?

Keep track of the names of the objects you find in the spaces below.

_ _ _ _   _ _ _ _ _ _

_ _ _ _   _ _ _ _

_ _ _ _ _   _ _ _ _

_ _ _ _   _ _ _

Art by Brian White

MAGICAL OCEAN MAZE

Find the path from START to FINISH. Then find the bell, mermaid, message in a bottle, fish, and open treasure chest.

START

FINISH

Art by Matt Lyon

GARAGE SALE MEMORY

Quick! Study this page for 60 seconds.
Then go to the top of the next page to test your memory.

Art by Dennis Jones

TEST YOUR MEMORY

Did you study the scene on the previous page? Now see if you can answer these questions. Circle your responses. No peeking!

1 What color is the cat? ORANGE BROWN BLACK

2 How many people are in the scene? 3 4 5

3 What does the sign say?

GARAGE SALE TODAY! WELCOME! OPEN!

4 What pattern is on the girl's yellow shirt?

5 Which two musical instruments are in the scene?

XYLOPHONE KEYBOARD GUITAR

EMOJI ADDITION

Each vehicle emoji has a value from 1 to 9. No two vehicles have the same value. Use the equations to figure out which number goes with each vehicle. The truck has the largest number and the motorcycle has the smallest number.

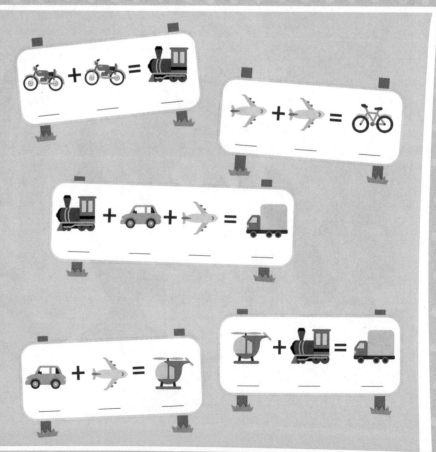

SEA SEARCH

There's an impostor hiding in this sea of fish. It has eight arms and can change color. Can you find it in the picture?

BONUS
Can you also find one sea creature with a snout, one with claws, and one with flippers, as well as 12 hidden shells?

Art by Travis Foster

A FIND IN THE FOREST

While Ray studies this cool lizard, look for hidden objects! First use the clues below to figure out the words. Each word is a hidden object to find in the big scene. Once you've found the 16 hidden objects, transfer the letters with numbers into the correct spaces on the next page to learn the answer to the riddle.

1. A _____ and thread

   __ __ __ __ __
   10

2. A cold treat in an edible container

   __ __ __ _ __ __ __ __ __ __ __ __ __
            5   2

3. This is attached to the side of a firetruck.

   __ __ __ __ __ __
   16   11

4. An erasable writing tool

   __ __ __ __ __ __
        8

5. Inches and centimeters are marked on this tool.

   __ __ __ __ __
   20

6. Cartoons slip on this fruit's peel.

   __ __ __ __ __ __
   3

7. Something you are proud to wave at the Olympics

   __ __ __ __
         13

8. The shape of a valentine

   __ __ __ __ __
   19   1

9. It sweeps up crumbs.

   __ __ __ __ __ __
            17

10. This is fun to fly in the sky on windy days.

    __ __ __ __
          4

11. Salmon or tuna

    __ __ __ __
       14

12. You can order yours plain or with lots of toppings.

    __ __ __ __ __
             9

13. It's helpful to have this when eating soup.

    __ __ __ __ __
          6

14. A fruit that's skinny on top and wider at the bottom

    __ __ __ __
    15

15. You may drink hot cocoa out of this.

    __ __ __
    7   12

16. You might see one shooting across the night sky.

    __ __ __ __
          18

Art by Paula Bossio

Why did the egg go into the jungle?

— — — — — — — — — — — — — — — — — — — — — .
1　2　　3　4　5　6　7　8　　9　10　　11　12　13　　14　15　16　17　18　19　20

X MARKS THE SPOT

All set for an eXciting cross-country trip? The 35 words listed here all contain the letter X. They fit into the grid in just one way. Use the number of letters in each word as a clue to its eXact spot in the grid. We know you'll eXcel at this!

3 LETTERS
AXE
BOX
FOX
SIX

4 LETTERS
EXAM
EXIT
FLEX
NEXT
OXEN
TAXI
TEXT
X-RAY

5 LETTERS
EXACT
EXTRA
HELIX
RELAX
TEXAS
XENON

6 LETTERS
EXCESS
EXCUSE
EXHALE
EXPECT
MEXICO

7 LETTERS
EXHIBIT
EXPLORE
EXPRESS
EXTREME
MAXIMUM
TEXTILE

9 LETTERS
EXCELLENT
EXCURSION
SAXOPHONE
XYLOPHONE

10 LETTERS
EXPERIMENT

13 LETTERS
EXTRAORDINARY

196

Art by Peter Grosshauser

TAKE A DIP

Hot summer afternoons bring crowds to the town pool. Can you find the 12 objects or actions that rhyme with DIP?

PICNIC POST

This picnic has more than just food. There are also 20 hidden envelopes. Can you find them all?

NEST QUEST

There are 14 eggs in these grids. Using the directions and hints below, can you figure out where all the eggs go?

Look at the grids. Each numbered square tells you how many of the empty squares touching it (above, below, left, right, or diagonally) contain an egg. Write an X on squares that can't have an egg. Then write an E on squares that have an egg.

HINTS:

- An egg cannot go in a square that has a number.

- In both grids, start by putting an X in all four of the squares touching the zero square. That will give you three squares to put in eggs that are around the square numbered 3.

- Remember that eggs can only go in squares that touch a numbered square.

This grid has 4 eggs.

	1	0	
3		2	
	2		1

This grid has 10 eggs.

		1		1
4				
		2		2
4		3		
		2		3
2				0

SUPER CHALLENGE!

So many food trucks to choose from for lunch. Which one will you try? Without clues or knowing what to look for, can you find the 25 hidden objects in this scene?

BUGGING OUT

All the ladybugs but one look exactly alike. Can you find the one unique bug?

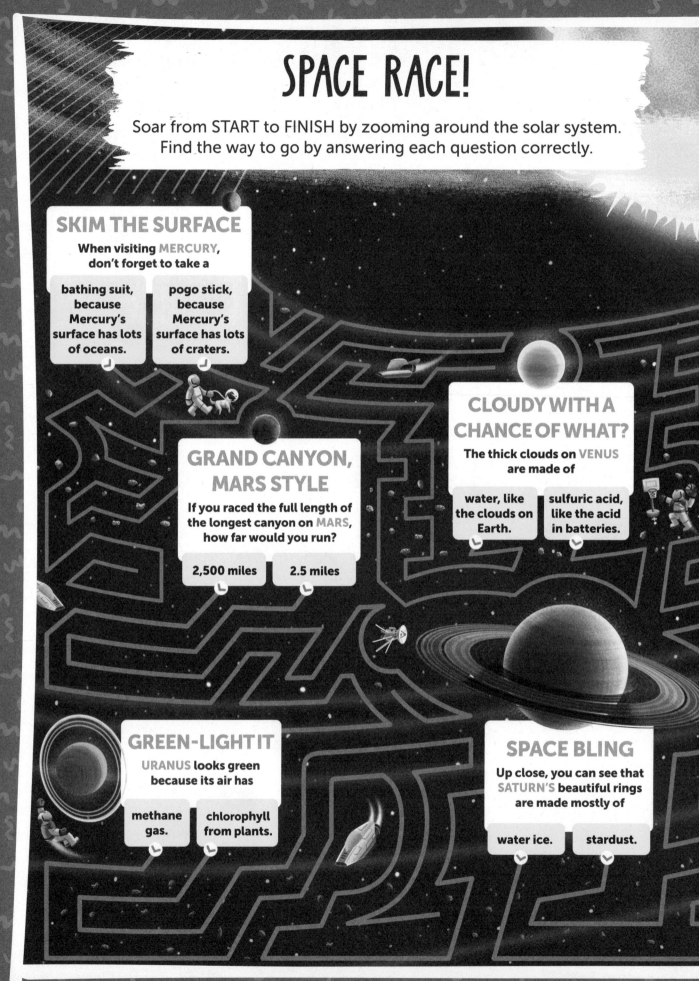

SPACE RACE!

Soar from START to FINISH by zooming around the solar system.
Find the way to go by answering each question correctly.

SKIM THE SURFACE

When visiting MERCURY,
don't forget to take a

bathing suit, because Mercury's surface has lots of oceans.

pogo stick, because Mercury's surface has lots of craters.

GRAND CANYON, MARS STYLE

If you raced the full length of the longest canyon on MARS, how far would you run?

2,500 miles

2.5 miles

CLOUDY WITH A CHANCE OF WHAT?

The thick clouds on VENUS are made of

water, like the clouds on Earth.

sulfuric acid, like the acid in batteries.

GREEN-LIGHT IT

URANUS looks green because its air has

methane gas.

chlorophyll from plants.

SPACE BLING

Up close, you can see that SATURN'S beautiful rings are made mostly of

water ice.

stardust.

START

STAR LIGHT, STAR SO BRIGHT

How does the SUN make so much light? Tons of

solar-powered light bulbs

Nuclear reactions

AUGUST AWESOMENESS

Every August, particles hit EARTH's air and burn up, creating the Perseid meteor shower. These particles come from

a comet.

the Moon.

STILL STORMY

For more than 100 years, JUPITER has had a storm bigger than Earth itself. The storm is called the

Great Red Spot.

Orange Giant.

GOING IN CIRCLES?

Start the stopwatch! It takes this long for NEPTUNE to go once around the Sun:

365 days

165 years

MOON COUNT

How many moons go around little PLUTO?

Five

None

FINISH

Art by Josh Lewis

205

LEAF PATTERNS

Find each pattern below in the grid.

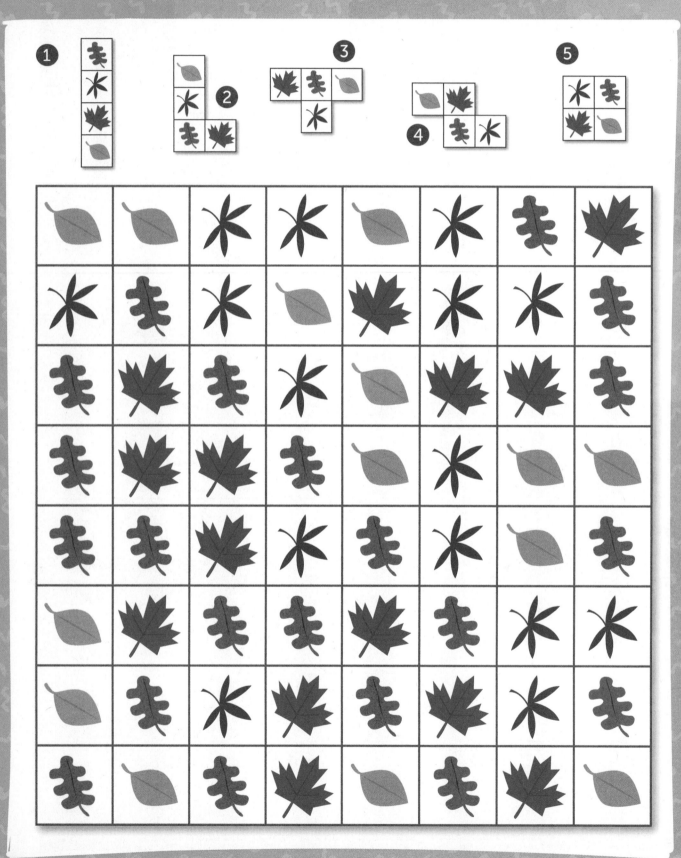

ONE PAW–SOME PARADE

Before the parade passes by, see if you can find 6 wheels, 6 waving hands, 6 bubbles, 6 bells, 4 number 6s, and the word *June* written 6 times.

Art by Kelly Kennedy

6 BY SIX

Each of these small scenes contains 6 hidden objects from the list below. Some objects are hidden in more than one scene. Can you find the 6 hidden objects in each scene?

HIDDEN OBJECT LIST

artist's brush (3)
canoe (3)
heart (3)
ladder (3)
lollipop (3)
mitten (3)
mug (2)
needle (4)
pencil (4)
rolling pin (4)
snake (2)
wedge of lemon (2)

BONUS
Two scenes contain the exact same set of hidden objects. Can you find that matching pair?

The numbers tell you how many times each object is hidden.

Art by Brian Michael Weaver

GOING IN CIRCLES

Go around and around using the clues to fill in the spaces. The last letter of each word will also be the first letter of the next word.

1. An Australian hopper
8. An egg is this shape.
11. A green citrus fruit
14. Opposite of late
18. 365 days
21. Garbage
27. Wife's partner
33. *T. rex* or *Dimetrodon*
40. A bunny
45. The Lone Star State
49. As _____ as a mule
56. Coin worth less than a dime
61. Baby sheep
64. Cross between breakfast and lunch
69. Often served with fries
77. A place to ice-skate
80. Make tea in it
85. London, _____
91. Porpoise's cousin
97. A bird's home
100. Underground passageway
105. A type of bean
108. Good-bye in Spanish

Why didn't the square talk to the circle?

Because there wasn't a point.

MOUSE MISCHIEF

Long live the mouse king! While these mice have a royally good time in the toy castle, see if you can find the 14 hidden objects in the scene below.

Now look for 10 differences between the nearly identical scenes on these two pages.

Art by Nuno Alexandre Vieira

FEELING ANTSY

There are 30 ant words hidden in the grid. For each one, the word ANT has been replaced by 🐜. Crawl up, down, across, backward, and diagonally to find as many as you can.

WORD LIST

antELOPE
antENNA
antIDOTE
antIQUE
antLERS
antSY
BRILLIant
CHant
CONSTant
CROISSant
DISTant
EGGPLant
ELEGant
ELEPHant
FantASY

FRAGRant
GALLant
Glant
HYDRant
IMMIGRant
IMPORTant
INFant
INSTant
PAGEant
PHEASant
SERGEant
SLant
TARantULA
VACant
Want

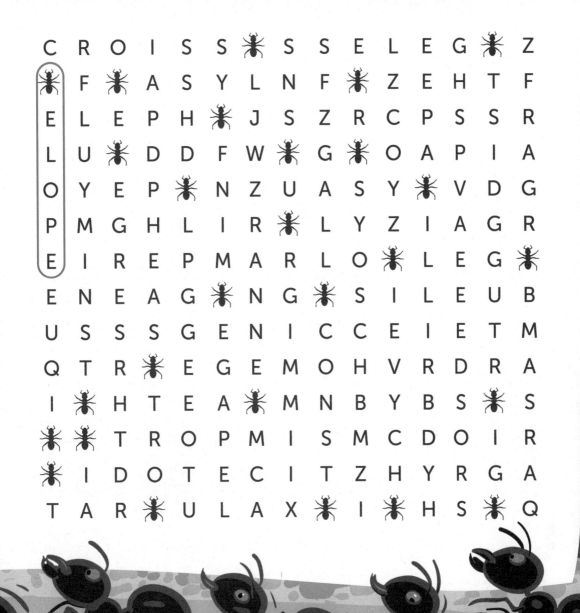

Art by Dave Clegg

WORDS AND OBJECTS

Pancakes for everyone! There are 8 WORDS hidden on this page that match the 8 OBJECTS hidden on the next page. Can you find them all?

Keep track of the names of the objects you find in the spaces below.

_ _ _ _ _ _ _ _ _ _   _ _ _ _ _ _ _ _ _ _

_ _ _ _ _   _ _ _ _ _ _ _

_ _ _ _ _ _ _   _ _ _ _ _ _ _ _ _ _ _ _ _

_ _ _ _ _   _ _ _ _ _ _ _ _ _ _ _

Art by Kevin Rechin

217

SPELUNKING SPLENDOR

People who visit this cave add their signatures on the wall. Help these spelunkers get from START to FINISH so they can add their signatures to the wall, too. Then see if you can find space to add your own signature to the wall.

START

HOUSE HUNT

The geography club is having its first meeting at River's house. He gave the club members the following directions. Can you find his house?

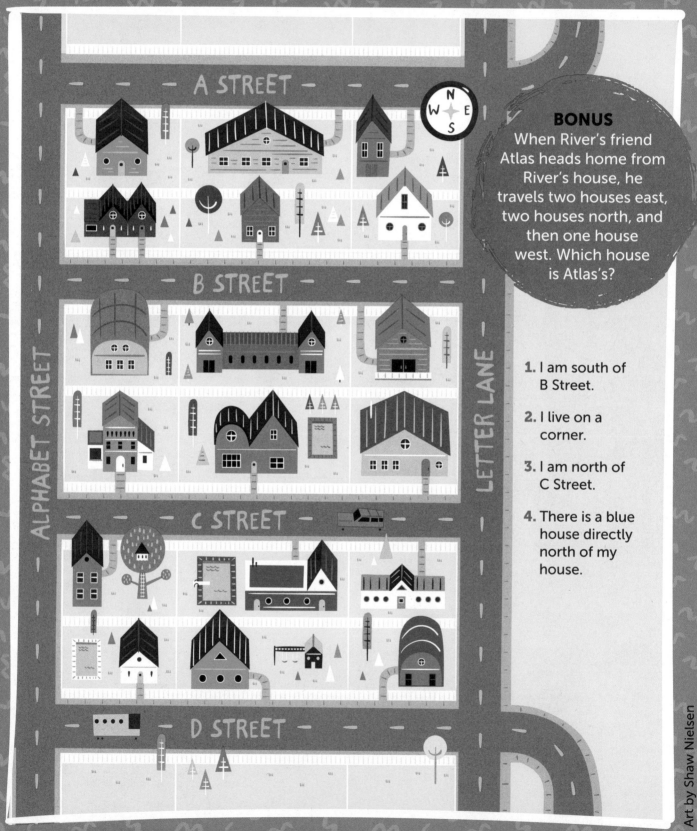

BONUS
When River's friend Atlas heads home from River's house, he travels two houses east, two houses north, and then one house west. Which house is Atlas's?

1. I am south of B Street.

2. I live on a corner.

3. I am north of C Street.

4. There is a blue house directly north of my house.

Art by Shaw Nielsen

CAT CITY MEMORY

Quick! Study this page for 60 seconds. Then go to the top of the next page to test your memory. Be on the lookout for a hidden puzzle piece!

Art by Brian Michael Weaver

TEST YOUR MEMORY

Did you study the scene on the previous page? Now see if you can answer these questions. Circle your responses. No peeking!

1 How many cats are in the taxi?   2   3   1

2 What is the waiter serving at the restaurant?
CHICKEN   FISH   ICE CREAM

3 What is the correct color of the bus driver's cap?

4 How many dogs are riding the bus (not counting the driver)?   7   8   9

5 Where is the hidden puzzle piece?
ON THE BUS   ON A CAT   ON THE STREET

SLOTH–LAND ADVENTURE PARK

Snoozanne wants to see a concert, Snorbert can't wait to go on a tube tour, and Dozalita is eager to try the ropes course. But all three activities have just started! What time is it?

ROCK-A-BYE CONCERTS
Every 3 hours from 12:00 P.M. to 9:00 P.M.

LAZY RIVER TUBE TOURS
Every 1½ hours from 12:00 P.M. to 9:00 P.M.

TREETOP ROPES COURSE
Every 2 hours from 2:00 P.M. to 8:00 P.M.

ROCK CONCERT

Can you find a beach ball, a hot dog, a striped hat, 4 pairs of twin dinos, a backpack, a red flag, an ice-cream cone, a green T-shirt, 3 baseball caps, a watermelon, and a pink chair?

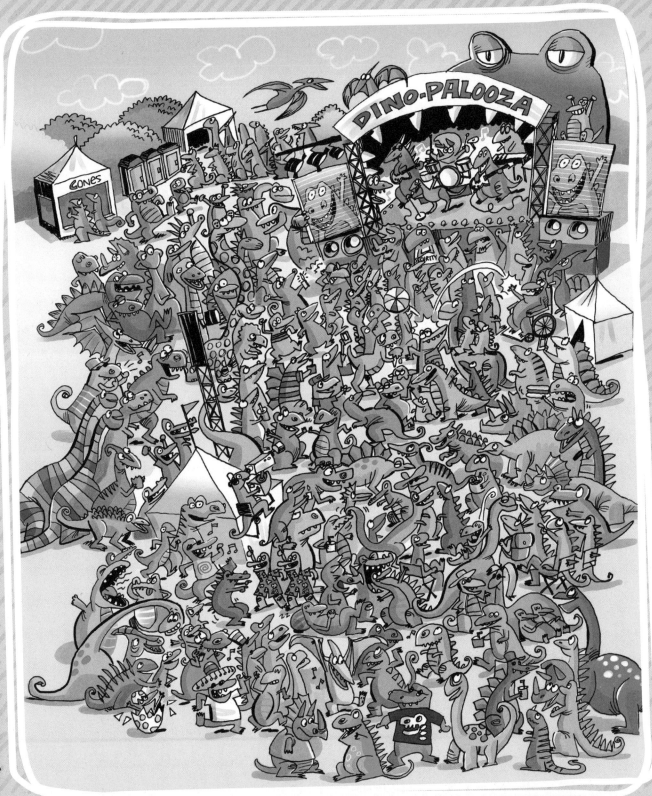

CRANBERRY BOG

Grab a rake and throw on your waders. It's time to harvest the cranberries.
First use the secret code to figure out what objects are hidden in the scene.
Then use the list to find the 17 hidden objects in the big picture.

CODE CRACKER

Each letter in the code is the letter in the alphabet that comes before the real letter. So, for example, an A in the code would signify that the letter is really a B. And the code word CNF would stand for DOG. Also, in this code, a Z stands for an A.

1. V Q D M B G — W R E N C H

2. B E L L

3. A N N L D Q Z M F

4. Q T K D Q

5. V D C F D   N E

6. D M U D K N O D

7. R K H B D   N E

8. C N L H M N

9. T L A Q D K K Z

10. O D M B H K

11. L T F

12. R Z V

13. G N Q R D R G N D

14. G D Z Q S

15. R Z H K A N Z S

16. R T M F K Z R R F R

17. C Q T L R S H B J

224

225

DANCE PARTY

It's time to get your groove on! We've rounded up 31 types of dances that fit into this grid in only one way. Use the number of letters in each word as a clue to where it might fit. Can you get them all before the song ends?

3 LETTERS
TAP

4 LETTERS
CLOG
JIVE
LINE
REEL

5 LETTERS
BELLY
BREAK
CONGA
DISCO
POLKA
RUMBA
SAMBA
SWING
TANGO
TWIST
WALTZ

6 LETTERS
BALLET
BOLERO
CONTRA
HIP-HOP
MINUET
SQUARE

7 LETTERS
FOXTROT
TWO-STEP

8 LETTERS
FANDANGO
FLAMENCO
IRISH JIG

9 LETTERS
CHA CHA CHA

10 LETTERS
CHARLESTON
MODERN JAZZ
TARANTELLA

MICROSCOPIC SEARCH

This micrograph of a wood cell is hiding 26 bowling pins. Can you find them all?

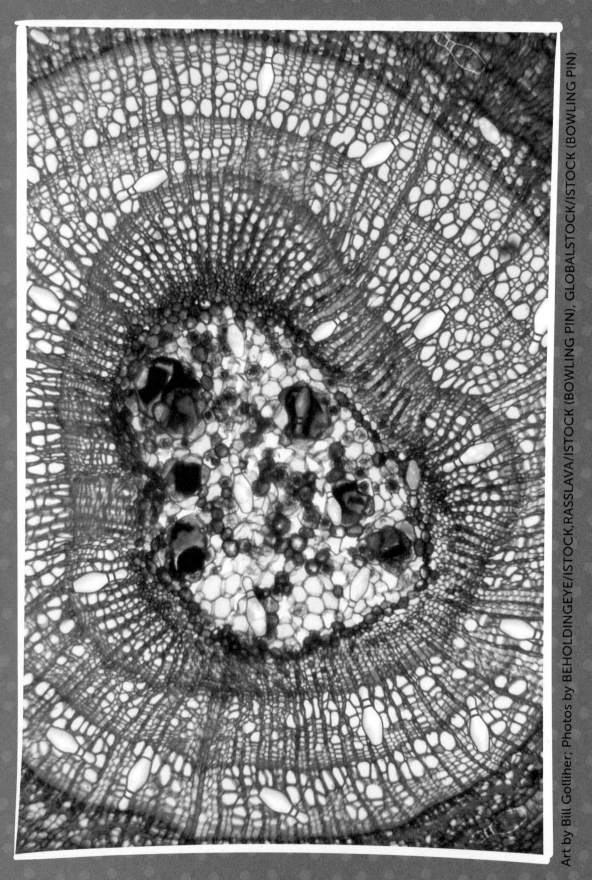

Art by Bill Golliher; Photos by BEHOLDINGEYE/ISTOCK,RASSLAVA/ISTOCK (BOWLING PIN), GLOBALSTOCK/ISTOCK (BOWLING PIN), ISTOCK (BOWLING PIN)

RIDDLE SUDOKU

Fill in the squares so the six letters appear only once in each row, column, and 2 × 3 box. Then read the highlighted squares to find the answer to each riddle.

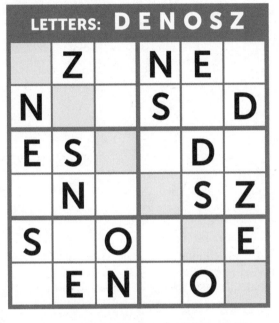

LETTERS: D E N O S Z

	Z		N	E	
N			S		D
E	S				D
	N			S	Z
S		O			E
	E	N		O	

A word I know, six letters it contains. Subtract just one, and 12 is what remains.

ANSWER: —— —— —— —— —— —— .

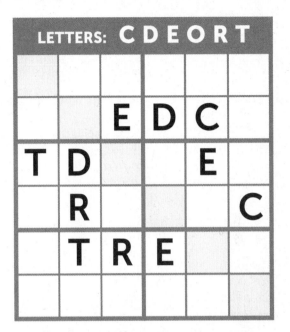

LETTERS: C D E O R T

		E		D	C
T	D			E	
	R				C
	T	R	E		

When sneezes, wheezes, and coughs make it difficult to cope, I will listen to you breathe with my trusty stethoscope.

ANSWER: —— —— —— —— —— —— .

RHYMING DEFINITIONS

It's time for some rhymes! Can you match each definition with the pair of rhyming words it describes?

1. Tool from Paris _____ A. Jelly deli
2. A do-nothing flower _____ B. Mountain fountain
3. Chocolate at the beach _____ C. Muddy buddy
4. High-altitude geyser _____ D. Lazy daisy
5. Spilled OJ _____ E. Green queen
6. Athlete's footwear _____ F. Morning warning
7. Jam store _____ G. Dove glove
8. Seasick royalty _____ H. French wrench
9. Alarm clock _____ I. Loose juice
10. Dirty friend _____ J. Quick lick
11. Bird's baseball mitt _____ K. Sandy candy
12. A tiny lollipop _____ L. Jock sock

WHAT'S THE WEATHER?

START

Better Bolt

Is it safe to stand under a tree during a thunderstorm?

Yes. Lightning is afraid of trees.

No way! Lightning might hit the tree. Seek shelter inside instead.

A Very Cool Place

Which of the 50 states has the lowest temperature on record at 80 degrees below zero?

Alaska

Montana

Torna-Do's and Don'ts

If a tornado is coming, you should

politely ask it to go away.

go underground into a basement or storm cellar. Or go to a small room with no windows on the lowest level.

Tons of Sun

True or false: It never rains in the desert.

True. That's what makes it a desert.

False. It rains—just not as often as it does in other places.

What's in a Cloud?

Cirrus clouds are white, feathery clouds high up in the atmosphere. They're made mostly of

cotton.   ice crystals.

The forecast says you can make it through this maze! Breeze from START to FINISH by answering each question correctly.

Hunt for Hues

The sun has come out, but it's still raining. In which direction should you look for a rainbow?

Toward the pot of gold

In the opposite direction of the sun

Snow Way!

One inch of rain has about as much water as

10 inches of snow.

a 1/2 inch of snow.

Too Many Twisters

Of all the countries in the world, which gets the most tornadoes?

The United States

China

Cloud Around

Cumulus comes from a Latin word that means "heap." Cumulus clouds are

puffy white clouds that look like cotton candy.

gray clouds shaped like pancakes.

Flash or Crash?

Which comes first, lightning or thunder?

Lightning

Thunder

FINISH

231

DILL IN THE BLANKS

There are 14 pickle slices in these grids. Using the directions and hints below, can you figure out where all the pickles go?

Look at the grids. Each numbered square tells you how many of the empty squares touching it (above, below, left, right, or diagonally) contain a pickle. Write an X on squares that can't have a pickle. Then write a P on squares that have a pickle.

HINTS:

- A pickle cannot go in a square that has a number.

- Put an X on all the squares touching a zero.

- Even if you're not sure where to put all the pickles around a number, fill in the ones you are sure of.

This grid has 4 pickles.

1	2	1	
2	4	2	

This grid has 10 pickles.

0			4		1
	1				2
			1		
	2				
2			2		3

CATS AND DOGS

Can you find 15 items or shapes that appear in both scenes?

Art by Kelly Kennedy

SUPER CHALLENGE!

At Bug University, insects take all kinds of cool courses! Without clues or knowing what to look for, can you find all 25 objects in the scene?

BONUS
Can you also find 3 hummingbirds in this scene?

ANSWERS

PAGE 5

PAGES 6–7

PAGE 8

PAGE 10

Top of Page
1. 2
2. WAITING IN LINE
3. SPONGE
4. PINK
5. ON A TURTLE'S SHELL

Bottom of Page
HOUSE 1 = 112 miles per week.
HOUSE 2 = 110 miles per week.
HOUSE 3 = 74 miles per week.
HOUSE 4 = 116 miles per week.

Mr. and Mrs. Melody should move to House 3 to travel the fewest miles each week.

PAGE 11

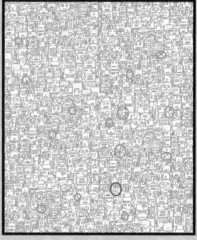

PAGES 12–13

1. mitten
2. crescent moon
3. slice of bread
4. needle
5. ruler
6. envelope
7. crown
8. heart
9. artist's brush
10. slice of pizza
11. wedge of lemon
12. flashlight
13. egg

What kind of tree has hands?
A PALM TREE.

What kind of soda do trees drink?
ROOT BEER.

PAGES 14–15

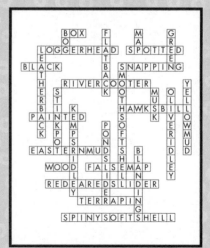

ANSWERS

PAGES 16–17

PAGES 18–19

1. String
2. Sing
3. Wing
4. King
5. Swing
6. Sling
7. Ring
8. Cling
9. Sting

PAGE 20

1	SO	X	SO
X	1	X	1
1	X	1	X
SO	2	SO	X

2	SO	X	O	X	1
X	SO	X	X	X	SO
1	X	4	SO	X	1
X	X	SO	SO	X	X
1	X	2	X	4	SO
SO	X	X	X	SO	SO

PAGE 21

PAGES 22–23

PAGES 24–25

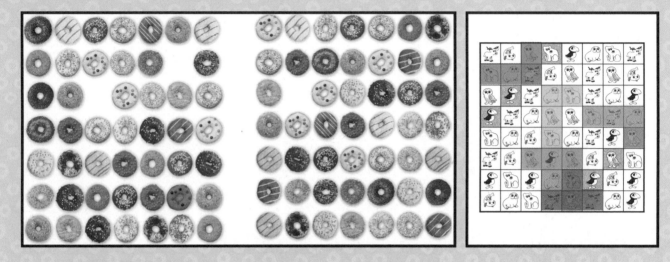

PAGE 26

PAGE 27

PAGES 28–29

PAGES 30–31

PAGES 32–33

ANSWERS

PAGES 34-35

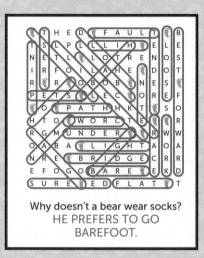

Why doesn't a bear wear socks?
HE PREFERS TO GO BAREFOOT.

PAGES 36—37

PAGES 38—39

PAGE 40

Here is the path we found.
You may have found others.

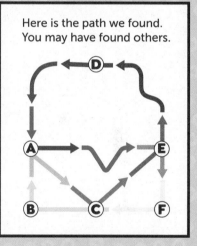

PAGE 42

Top of Page

1. 2
2. THE ROCKETS
3. ORANGE
4. 3
5. ON THE SPACESHIP

Bottom of Page

Anita sold 56 bags of pitas
and made $224.00.

BONUS

PAGE 43

ANSWERS

PAGES 44–45

1. can
2. candy cane
3. ice cream cone
4. button
5. airplane
6. spoon
7. apple
8. light bulb
9. magnifying glass
10. fork
11. clock
12. wedge of lemon
13. crown
14. banana
15. glove
16. ruler
17. magic lamp
18. envelope

PAGES 46–47

PAGE 48

PAGE 49

Top of Page

Letters: ILEOKN

O	N	E	L	K	I
K	I	L	E	N	O
E	K	N	O	I	L
L	O	I	K	E	N
N	E	O	I	L	K
I	L	K	N	O	E

What does a pig call its mother's brother? OINKLE.

Letters: ARHESO

H	R	E	S	A	O
A	O	S	H	E	R
R	H	A	E	O	S
E	S	O	R	H	A
O	E	R	A	S	H
S	A	H	O	R	E

What do you call a sick pony? A little HOARSE.

Bottom of Page

1. A SHEEP.
2. A ROOSTER.

PAGE 50

UFO	X	3	UFO
2	UFO	UFO	2
X	2	X	X
0	X	X	0

UFO	1	X	X	X	1
X	X	X	2	X	UFO
2	UFO	UFO	UFO	X	1
X	UFO	6	UFO	4	X
X	X	X	UFO	UFO	2
0	X	1	X	3	UFO

PAGE 51

BONUS: SCARF

PAGES 52–53

240

ANSWERS

PAGES 54—55

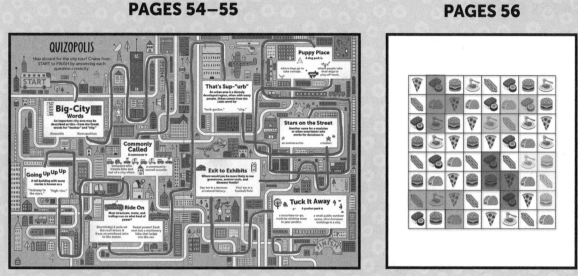

PAGES 56

PAGE 57

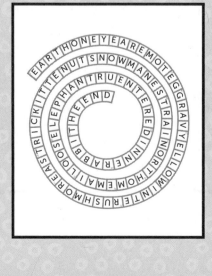

PAGE 58—59

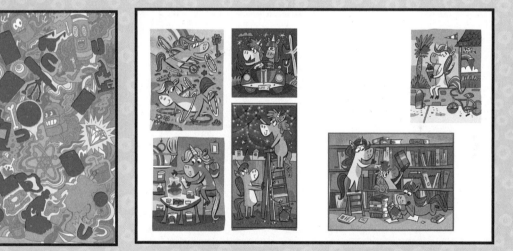

PAGES 60—61

PAGES 62—63

ANSWERS

PAGES 64–65

1. DOG: Donkey Organizing Glasses
2. BEE: Beavers Eating Eggs
3. ANT: Astronaut Numbering Tubas
4. PIG: Pandas Interviewing Goldfish
5. CAT: Camels Adoring Turtles
6. BAT: Bears Acting Tired
7. RAT: Rabbits Arresting Turkeys
8. EEL: Elephant Elevating Limousine
9. COW: Crabs Ordering Waffles

PAGES 66–67

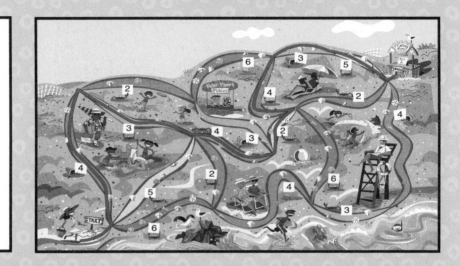

PAGES 68–69

PAGE 70

PAGE 72

Top of Page
1. 3
2. RUFFFF
3. YELLOW / GREEN
4. MOUNTAINS
5. BETWEEN TREES

Bottom of Page
What do you call dough used for making dog biscuits? COLLIE FLOUR.

PAGE 73

ANSWERS

PAGES 74–75

1. nail
2. horseshoe
3. ship
4. banana
5. conch shell
6. wishbone
7. ladder
8. carrot
9. bell
10. fan
11. doughnut
12. die

How do ghosts take their eggs?
TERRI-FRIED.

What's a pirate ghost's favorite kind of tea?
BOO-TEA.

PAGES 76–77

PAGES 78–79

PAGES 80–81

Trivia Answer:
IT ISN'T A STAR AT ALL.
IT'S A METEOR.

PAGE 82

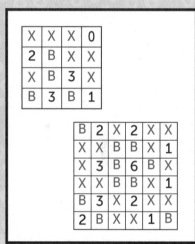

PAGE 83

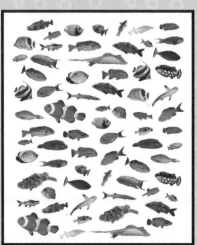

PAGES 84–85

ANSWERS

PAGES 86–87

PAGE 88

PAGE 89

PAGES 90–91

PAGES 92–93

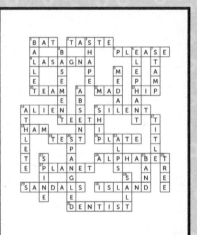

PAGES 94–95

244

ANSWERS

PAGE 96

Top of Page

Letters: A C H L N U

L	U	H	C	N	A
N	A	C	H	U	L
H	N	U	L	A	C
C	L	A	N	H	U
U	H	L	A	C	N
A	C	N	U	L	H

What's an astronaut's favorite meal? LAUNCH.

Letters: O T E R C K

R	K	T	E	C	O
C	O	E	R	T	K
K	R	C	T	O	E
T	E	O	K	R	C
O	T	K	C	E	R
E	C	R	O	K	T

What only starts to work after it's fired? A ROCKET.

Bottom of Page

1. TEA
2. AIR
3. EEL
4. LIAR
5. TALE
6. ALIEN
7. START
8. RAIN

PAGE 97

Xu changed elevators four times. After riding the orange elevator to floor 5, Xu returned to the ground floor to change to the blue elevator. He rode the blue elevator to floors 4 and then 2, changed to orange for floor 3, changed to blue for floor 6, and changed to orange for floor 7.

PAGES 98–99

PAGE 100

PAGE 102

Top of Page

1. 3
2. WRITING NOTES
3. BLUE
4. AN OCTOPUS
5. ON THE GREEN FISH

Bottom of Page

1. $3.30 3. $2.40
2. $4.00 4. $4.80

BONUS
Poppy had 55 sheets of paper left.

PAGE 103

PAGES 104–105

1. BOOK
2. PARTY HAT
3. UMBRELLA
4. COMB
5. SLICE OF CAKE
6. CANOE
7. BROCCOLI
8. BOOMERANG
9. CUPCAKE
10. PICKAX
11. SAUCEPAN
12. DOMINO
13. MUSICAL NOTE
14. FISH
15. BANANA
16. HEART
17. TOOTHBRUSH
18. SNAKE
19. PENCIL
20. FISHHOOK

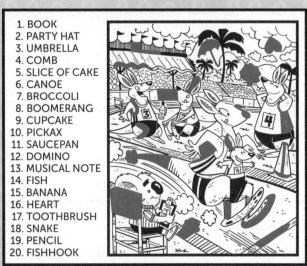

ANSWERS

PAGES 106–107

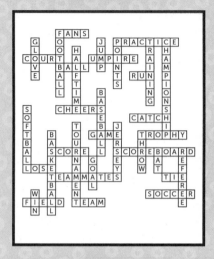

PAGES 108–109

PAGE 110

A seat has been replaced by a beet, a tire by a dryer, a kart by a heart, a traffic cone by a phone, a steering wheel by a banana peel, trees by skis, a hat by a cat, a two by a shoe, a flower by a shower, and a flag by a bag.

We found these things that rhyme with go. (You may have found others.) Buffalo, dough, crow, snow, hoe, bow, arrow, and banjo.

PAGE 111

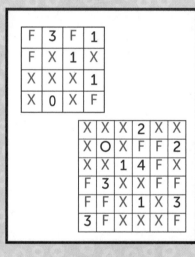

PAGES 112–113

PAGES 114–115

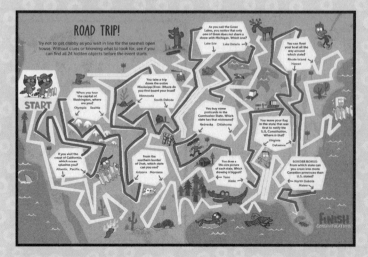

PAGE 116

ANSWERS

PAGE 117

PAGE 118

PAGE 119

Here are the animal names we found: cow, crow, cat, bat, bear, rat, crab, owl, tiger

PAGES 120—121

PAGES 122—123

PAGES 124—125

PAGES 126—127

Word Scramble Answers:
CRICKET.
SQUASH.

ANSWERS

PAGES 128–129

PAGE 130

PAGE 132

Top of Page
1. BLUE
2. 10
3. GO ANTS!
4. LADYBUG
5. ON THE WALL

Bottom of Page

🍿 = $8.00
🥨 = $6.00
🍭 = $3.00
⬛ = $5.00

PAGE 133

PAGES 134–135

1. SAILBOAT
2. SCREWDRIVER
3. LOLLIPOP
4. BOOT
5. WAFFLE
6. CANOE
7. LEAF
8. HOCKEY STICK
9. ARTIST'S BRUSH
10. OVEN MITT
11. BASEBALL BAT
12. FLASHLIGHT
13. BOOMERANG
14. SPATULA

Why is it better to eat doughnuts in the rain?
YOU GET MORE SPRINKLES.

PAGES 136–137

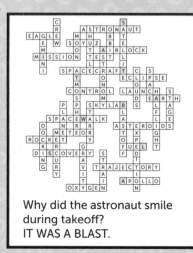

Why did the astronaut smile
during takeoff?
IT WAS A BLAST.

PAGES 138–139

248

ANSWERS

249

PAGE 140

Top of Page

LETTERS: A R N T S F

F	A	S	T	N	R
N	R	T	S	A	F
S	N	A	F	R	T
T	F	R	N	S	A
A	S	F	R	T	N
R	T	N	A	F	S

Where do insects go on vacation? FRANTS.

LETTERS: D P E R Y S

S	Y	R	E	D	P
E	P	D	R	Y	S
D	S	Y	P	R	E
R	E	P	D	S	Y
P	R	S	Y	E	D
Y	D	E	S	P	R

What do you call an undercover arachnid? SPYDER.

Bottom of Page

What did the itchy dog say to the flea? STOP BUGGING ME!

PAGE 141

PAGES 142–143

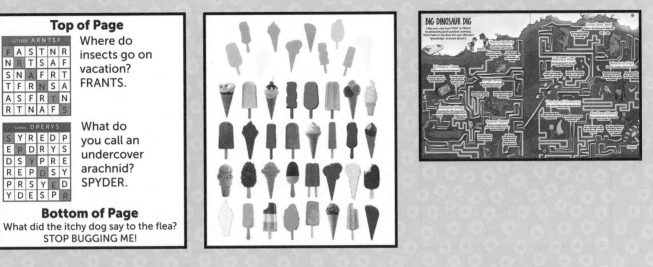

PAGE 144

PAGE 145

1	X	X	X
2	S	X	1
X	S	4	S
1	X	3	S

S	3	X	1	X	X
S	S	X	X	S	1
X	X	2	S	X	2
X	2	2	2	S	1
S	S	2	X	X	X
3	S	X	X	1	S

PAGE 146

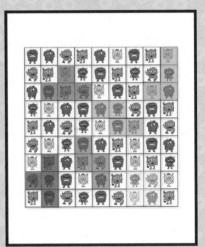

PAGE 147

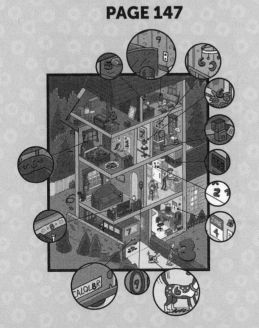

PAGES 148–149

ANSWERS

PAGES 150–151

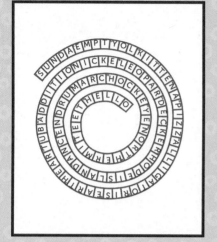

PAGES 152–153

PAGES 154–155

1. Arrow
2. Blow
3. Bow
4. Crow
5. Doe
6. Elbow
7. Marshmallow
8. Moe
9. Row
10. Sew
11. Show
12. Throw
13. Tow
14. Yo-yo
15. No
16. Pillow
17. Snow
18. Toe
19. Window

PAGES 156–157

PAGES 158–159

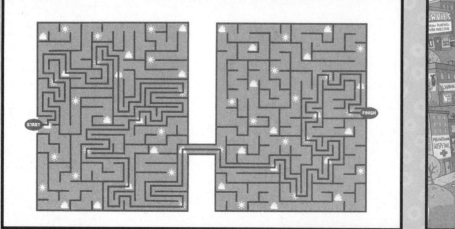

PAGE 160

Catrick will cross the bridge 6 times.

ANSWERS

PAGE 162

Top of Page

1. 9
2. A SPONGE
3. ORANGE
4. A TOWEL
5. IN A PUDDLE

Bottom of Page

Only odd numbers: blue.
Adds up to 19: red.
Highest score: yellow.
Lowest score: green.

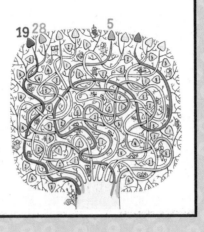

PAGE 163

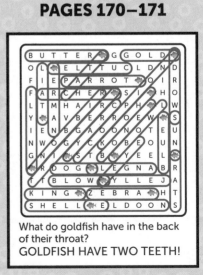

PAGES 164–165

1. BELL
2. FISH
3. KITE
4. TACK
5. YO-YO
6. CANOE
7. RULER
8. SCARF
9. BANANA
10. BASEBALL
11. ENVELOPE
12. FISHHOOK
13. ARTIST'S BRUSH
14. CRESCENT MOON
15. SLICE OF PIZZA
16. DRINKING STRAW

PAGES 166–167

PAGES 168–169

PAGES 170–171

What do goldfish have in the back of their throat?
GOLDFISH HAVE TWO TEETH!

ANSWERS

PAGE 172

1	CC	X	X
X	X	X	0
X	1	X	X
X	X	CC	1

1	X	X	CC	CC	2
CC	X	2	CC	4	CC
3	X	X	X	X	1
CC	CC	X	1	X	X
X	X	X	X	CC	3
0	X	X	2	CC	CC

PAGE 173

PAGES 174–175

PAGES 176–177

PAGE 178

PAGE 179

We found an apple, bear, cat, dog, elephant, fox, giraffe, hedgehog, iguana, jellyfish, kangaroo, lion, monkey, nest, ostrich, peacock, quail, rhinoceros, squirrel, ticket, unicorn, vulture, wheel, xylophone, yarn, and zebra. What else did you find?

PAGES 180–181

ANSWERS

PAGES 182–183

PAGES 184–185

PAGE 186

Top of Page

Letters: A C E H S W					
C	W	E	S	A	H
S	A	H	E	W	C
H	E	S	W	C	A
W	C	A	H	S	E
A	H	W	C	E	S
E	S	C	A	H	W

What did the nut say when it sneezed? "CASHEW!"

Letters: B I M R T U					
R	B	U	I	T	M
T	I	M	U	R	B
U	R	B	T	M	I
I	M	T	B	U	R
B	T	R	M	I	U
M	U	I	R	B	T

What did the frog say when he saw the bunny? "RIBBIT."

Bottom of Page

1. Emma planned the route.
2. We stopped to sketch at the bridge.
3. Two squirrels came racing along a log!
4. The whole crew ate raisins for energy.
5. We came upon chopped trees near a beaver dam.
6. Our pace had to slow at challenging, rocky parts of the trail.

PAGE 187

Rita owns Spa-Ghetti, Terry owns the Penne Candy Shoppe, Marty owns Blinguini Jewelry, and Zoey owns Pet-tuccine Groomers.

PAGES 188–189

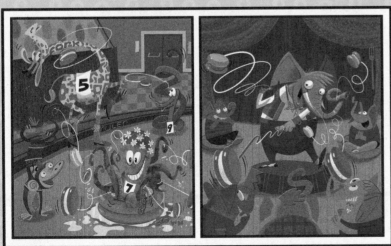

253

ANSWERS

PAGE 190

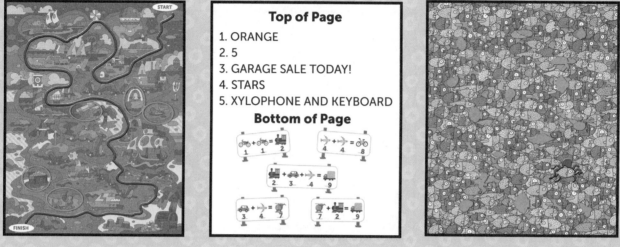

PAGE 192

Top of Page
1. ORANGE
2. 5
3. GARAGE SALE TODAY!
4. STARS
5. XYLOPHONE AND KEYBOARD

Bottom of Page

🛴 + 🏍 = 🚂
1   1   2

✈ + ✈ = 🚲
4   4   8

🚂 + 🚙 + ✈ = 🚌
2   3   4   9

🚙 + 🚲 = 🛴
3   4   7

🛴 + 🚂 = 🚌
7   2   9

PAGE 193

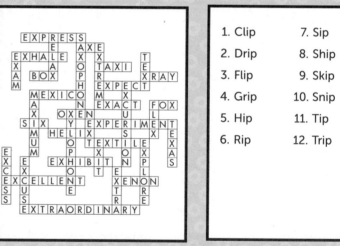

PAGES 194—195

1. NEEDLE
2. ICE-CREAM CONE
3. LADDER
4. PENCIL
5. RULER
6. BANANA
7. FLAG
8. HEART
9. BROOM
10. KITE
11. FISH
12. PIZZA
13. SPOON
14. PEAR
15. MUG
16. STAR

Why did the egg go into the jungle?
TO BECOME AN EGG-SPLORER.

PAGES 196—197

EXPRESS
E   AXE
EXHALE X X TAXI   T
X   A X   R   E
A BOX O P   E TEXRAY
M   M H EXPECT
      MEXICON M X
      A   X EXACT FOX
      X OXEN U L
      SIX Y EXPERIMENT
      M HELIX S X T
EXCESS U O   X   E
      M P TEXTILE   X
      E O X T E   A
EXCEL EXHIBIT X S
      L O   T E
EXCESS E EXCELLENT XENON
S   U   E   R
S   E EXTRAORDINARY

PAGE 198

1. Clip
2. Drip
3. Flip
4. Grip
5. Hip
6. Rip
7. Sip
8. Ship
9. Skip
10. Snip
11. Tip
12. Trip

PAGE 200

PAGE 201

X	1	0	X
E	X	X	X
3	E	2	E
E	2	X	1

E	E	1	X	E	1
4	X	X	X	X	X
E	E	2	X	X	2
4	X	3	E	E	E
E	E	2	X	3	X
2	X	X	X	O	X

PAGE 202

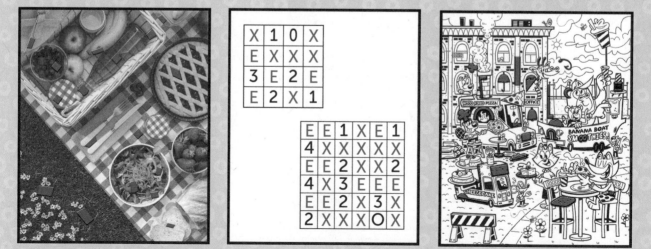

254

ANSWERS

PAGE 203

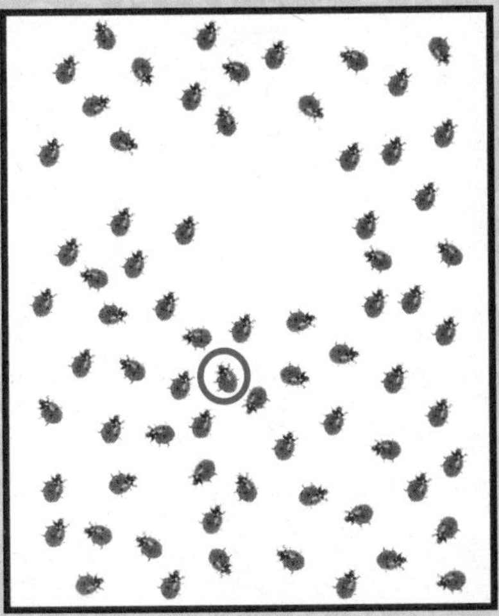

PAGES 204–205

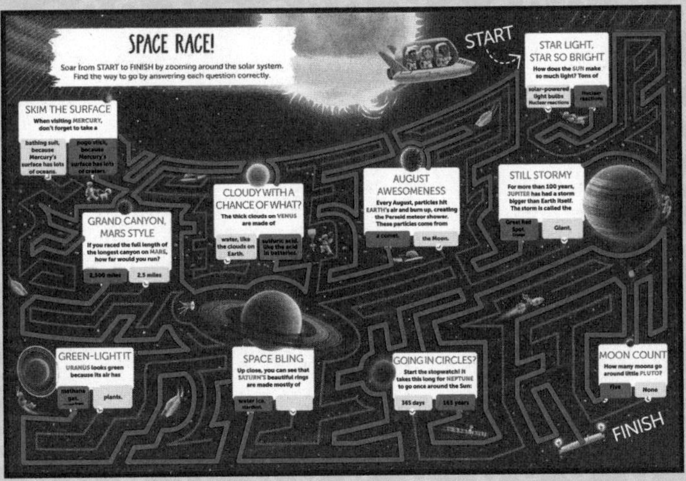

PAGE 206

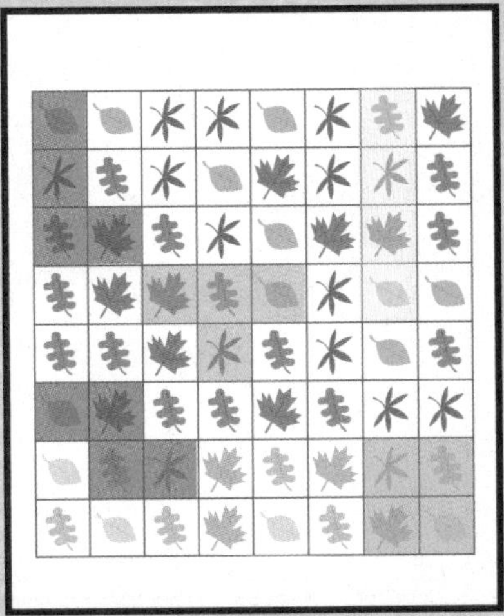

PAGE 207

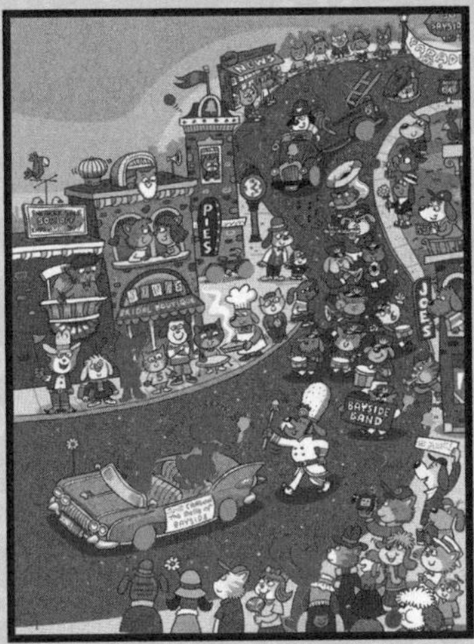

PAGES 208–209

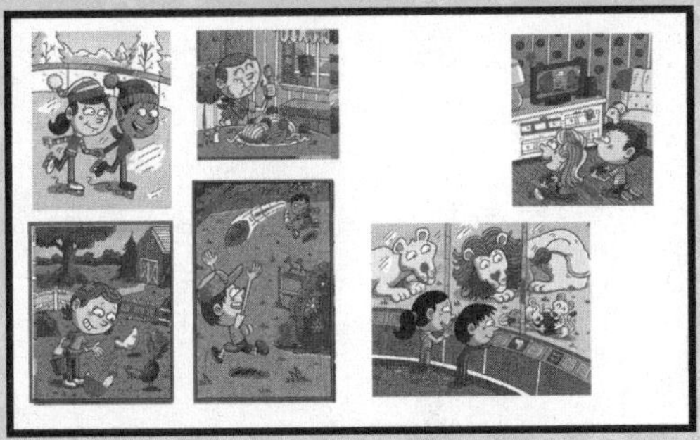

PAGES 210–211

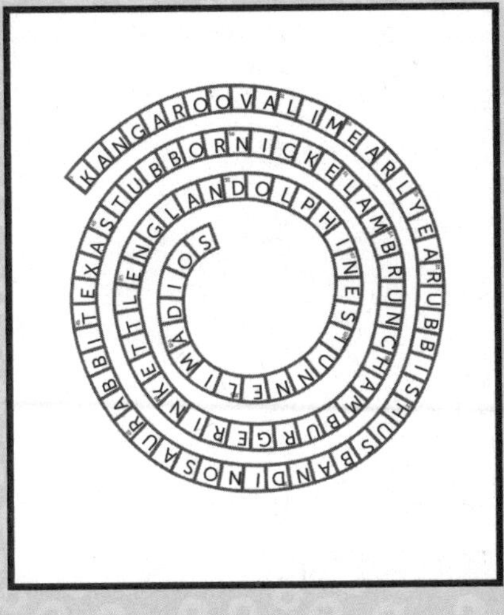

PAGES 212–213

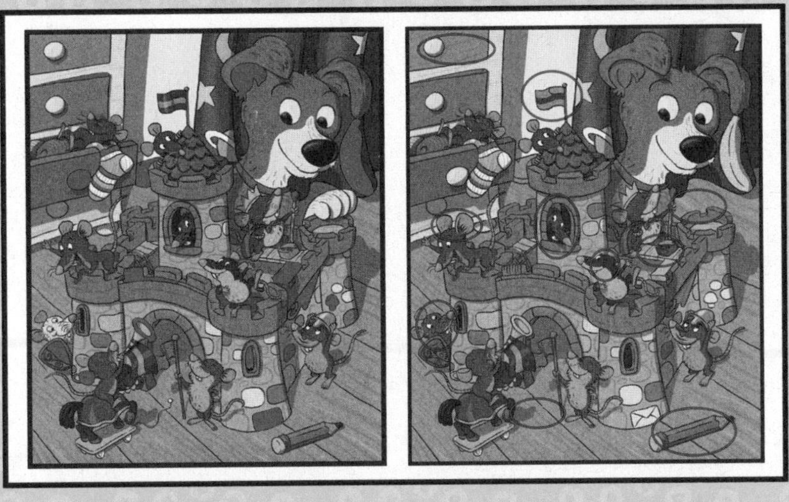

ANSWERS

PAGES 214–215

PAGES 216–217

PAGES 218–219

PAGE 220

River's House

Atlas's House

PAGE 222

Top of Page

1. 1
2. FISH
3. BLUE
4. 9
5. ON THE BUS

Bottom of Page

It is 6:00 p.m.

PAGE 223

PAGES 224–225

1. WRENCH
2. BELL
3. BOOMERANGE
4. RULER
5. WEDGE OF ORANGE
6. ENVELOPE
7. SLICE OF PIZZA
8. DOMINO
9. UMBRELLA
10. PENCIL
11. MUG
12. SAW
13. HORSESHOE
14. HEART
15. SAILBOAT
16. SUNGLASSES
17. DRUMSTICK

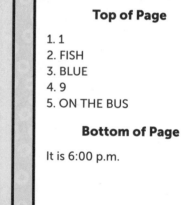

```
T E F R U I T F L Y Y L F E R I F
E E B U Z Z T S I L V E R F I S H
R B M N E T M E A L Y B U G O X K
M Y N Y S A L J N C R I C K E T L
I E U U C O C K R O A C H F G E
T N C L O D D R A G O N F L Y U A
E O F Y L F W O L B R H K P G B F
L H B G U B K N I T S V A H K Y H
E B E D B U G X A W Y U T O W D O
K L Y M B U T T E R F L Y U H A P
M A Y F L Y A V L S R X D S I L P
P D R O N E N V F M X V I E R E E
W A L K I N G S T I C K D F R O R
E W E E V I L E A N V I J L U T S
C A P H E E L G H C M S C Y G P I
H P R C V T D T O F I R E A N T T
I H X W E V O E G D I M D U D V N
R I T E I M O S Q U I T O H N A A
P D B Y P G R A S S H O P P E R M
```

127

BONUS:
Unscramble the letters to learn an insect's favorite sport.

R C K I E T C.

Unscramble the letters to find a veggie bugs hate.

Q S A S U H.

Art by Carolina Farias

WORDS AND OBJECTS

What a beautiful day for a bike ride! There are 8 WORDS hidden on this page that match the 8 OBJECTS hidden on the next page. Can you find them all?

Keep track of the names of the objects you find in the spaces below.

_ _ _ _   _ _ _ _ _ _

_ _ _ _   _ _ _ _ _

_ _ _ _ _   _ _ _

_ _ _   _ _ _ _ _ _ _ _

Art by Iryna Bodnaruk

129

ENCHANTED FOREST MAZE

Find a path from START to FINISH. Then find the woodpecker,
rabbit, fairy, and squirrel.

FINISH

START

Art by Matt Lyon